Rights of Way, the body as witness in public space

PREFACE

The movements of our individual and collective bodies through cities and space have long, complex histories. Despite the usual association of bodily movement with the everyday, the seemingly obvious, or, perhaps, even the mundane; when considered at length, our ability (or inability) to move through space and place transforms us from mere bystanders into activators and witnesses of our cities. As Rebecca Solnit demonstrates in her work *Wanderlust: A History of Walking*; bodily movement trespasses so readily through anatomy, anthropology, architecture, gardening, geography, political history, cultural history, literature, sexuality, religious studies, and more.[1]

To consider walking and movement from a historical perspective, the European flâneur, referred to as the 'botanist of the sidewalk'[2] and the 'painter of modern life',[3] has been understood in relation to the exploration and documentation of the complex political dynamics and societal changes happening in cities across Europe during the 19th Century. The flâneurs, note: typically European, white, middle class men, were city-street-strollers who perused, observed, experienced, and catalogued the direct surroundings, chance encounters, and sensory cues granted to them by their cityscapes. Through vivid descriptions and politically charged commentaries inspired by their countless walks, the inner-city workings and fraught political goings-on of Europe have been so well preserved.

From a more contemporary viewpoint, we can recognise the political significance of our bodily movements by looking to key social movements and activist campaigns that have gained momentum over the past decade. Demonstrations from *Occupy Wall Street, Pride, Women's March, Climate March, Reclaim the Night,* and *Black Lives Matter* aid us in acknowledging how our physical movements in public space are political forces to be reckoned with. The act of taking to the streets and moving as a communal body around neighborhoods and parks, along roads and streets, and through courtyards and squares in civil choreography, can be read as much a reclamation of space as an exercise in demanding our rights to citizenship. Through such gestures and movements, we activate our bodies as both a symbol and a tool for social, political, cultural, and economic change, to challenge the power-plays of the city, and redefine how we recognise, experience, and witness place and space.

Yet such access to public space and rights to roam are built upon long, established histories of violence and exclusion. The blue-prints of our cities are exchanged and agreed upon by architects, politicians, urban planners, and property developers who follow top-down, traditional narratives that perpetuate hegemonic cityscapes and promote arenas of exclusion, meaning individuals and groups continue to be systematically excluded, harassed, and violated as a result of their attempts to exist in such spaces. Therefore, with both the historical and the contemporary in mind, what the flâneur and far more recent social and political movements show us is the importance of the body as witness in public space.

Witnessing, when understood in its traditional form as a method of recollection or a symbol of the witness stand, typically grants authority to a select, privileged few, whilst acting as a mode of oppression against the powerless. Yet by moving away from an emphasis on the purely visual, and instead granting agency to the other senses, emotions, and lived experiences that look towards psychogeography as well as to the physicality and performativity of our bodies in space, active witnessing provides rich, complex, and inclusive understandings of our direct environments.

Such bodily witnessing continues to remain urgent as we grapple with the effects of shifting city borders, mass surveillance, tightening immigration controls, police brutality, technological advancements, precarious citizenship rights, widespread gentrification, divisive body politics, and limited access to public space, in the shaping of the streets and cities we move within. In an age where rising hate crimes and acts of violence regularly take place in public space, and when many must still campaign and protest to reclaim their stake in the public realm, *Rights of Way, the body as witness in public space* seeks to explore who has the rights of way to gather the past, the present, and the future of public space, to explore and envision varied forms of witnessing and access, and apply it to the cities and spaces in which we reside.

[1]
Rebecca Solnit *Wanderlust: A History of Walking,* Granta Books 2014

[2]
The Situationists and the City, edited by Tom Mcdonough, Verso 2010

[3]
ibid

Table of contents

The Evolution of Public Space

The Politics of Access

The Body as Witness

To speak of public space, we must begin with the body.

How do our movements shape our cities?

*How can public space respond to our
bodies, as sites of lived experience, where
identity, memory, and history interact
and inscribe themselves?*

*In what ways do we define the "publics"
of our public space?*

And who have the rights of way?

Rights of Way, the body as witness in public space explores questions around bodily movement and bodily witnessing as key factors in how we produce, and are produced in turn, by our cities and spaces, particularly through the mediums of testimony, allegory, and personal, lived experience. As a project, *Rights of Way* intended to understand public space by moving away from purely urban planning or architectural based approaches, to that of a more bodily-focussed perspective. In turn, aiming to perceive how our movements, experiences, senses, and body politic, allow for us to be witnesses and activators of our cities and public spaces.

In November 2020, the *Rights of Way* exhibition was presented at Onomatopee Projects in Eindhoven, the Netherlands, showcasing the works of nine local, national and international artists. All of the exhibiting artists were tasked with responding to their roles as witnesses in public space, especially in relation to the ways in which bodies are so often defined, or confined, when in such spaces. The result was a range of both newly commissioned and pre-existing works that encompassed the mediums of film, sound, interview, installation, performance and photography. Together, the works complicated, enriched, and broadened our understandings of public space as the meeting points between cities and bodies. For this publication, each of the exhibiting artists and collectives from the exhibition. Pauline Agustoni, Elia Castino, The Dazzle Club, Corinne Heyrman, Paoletta Holst, Shannon Finnegan, Alessandro Marchi, Jeannette Petrik and Soeria van den Wijngaard, alongside Kevin Gotkin, Annee Grøtte Viken, Rahma Khazam, and Christa-Maria Lerm Hayes, were invited to produce contributions that not only related to the works displayed during the exhibition, but also continued to expand upon the topic as a whole. In doing so, reflecting on how public space and its associated connections continue to evolve, offering new possibilities and challenges in the process.

From the view of this publication, public space is a composite of visible and invisible systems and structures, points of use and access, and live and evolving frameworks. Moreover, public space can be seen to contain and display manifold layers of social, political, economic, and cultural meaning. Charged, inhabited spaces that are produced and reproduced by its users, those who move along its lengths, and interact with its surfaces, who feel a sense of ease, or perhaps more commonly, unease, when present. It is important here to emphasise how vital *use* is in creating identity and meaning in these spaces that define our towns and cities. This idea is very much in line with Geographer Yi-Fu Tuan's assertion, "a space only becomes a place when, through movement, we invest it with meaning, when we see it as something to be perceived, apprehended, and experienced".[1] Which naturally ascertains the questions, *who* is the "we" who is able to move through such spaces? Who is granted access to invest a place with meaning? And, essentially, how "public" is our public space? Whose body has the right of way to exist in these zones, and whose does not?

These questions, surrounding the "publicness" of our public spaces, has long been a matter of contestation, from the days of the flâneur to the modern city dweller, and it lives on in the foundations of this publication. The two years of research and writing behind *Rights of Way* have offered particularly compelling moments to embark on such thinking, as during this same time period we have been plunged into globally facing political, economic, planetary, and health ruptures, which have demanded both our witnessing and our action. These tensions have simultaneously sparked outpouring onto streets, courtyards, and squares in protest, as much as they have the restriction and retreatment into our private spheres and homes. This period has been further marked by repeated cases of abhorrent violence that have taken place on streets, in parks, and in public spaces. The collective response to such senseless acts has prompted thousands to come together and take to the streets to protest, mourn, commemorate, and challenge the systems and structures of oppression that are deeply embedded in our societies. Public space has been a key player throughout this all. It has been

[1]
Tuan, Yi-fu. Space and place: the perspective of experience. Minneapolis: University of Minnesota Press, 1977

associated at once with our freedoms, in the fight for citizenship and the protection of life, and, at the same time, a heavily contested space of danger and fear, resulting in increased surveillance and restriction. What the past two years have therefore shown is that there are many ways to approach the topic of public space: fear, joy, danger, play, freedom, grief, aguish. Public space is charged with the personal and the political—but also with the bodily: our bodily movements, our bodily joys, our bodily strifes. Therefore, when speaking of public space, we must begin with the body.

In some cases, we can clearly identify whose body has the ability to, or is comfortable in, using public space, both by actively witnessing this when in public arenas, and also by asking critical questions around who is present, and who is not? Who is welcomed? Whose existence is surveyed and controlled? Often the power structures that determine the answers to these questions are more difficult to discern, embedded in decades, if not centuries, of hierarchy, power and exclusion that lie beneath the surface, and yet dictate and dominate how events upon the surface are played out. By continuing to question and challenge these systems, we are able to broaden the parameters of who can form the publics of our public spaces, and the very function these spaces hold. These are therefore the very questions and ruminations that formed the basis for the responses that have been collated in this publication, structured under three main sections.

The first section, The Evolution of Public Space, details the ways in which the changing nature of public space, and our evolving relationships with it can be documented through art, lived experience, and personal memoir. This section begins with a contribution from Christa-Maria Lerm-Hayes, who activates the writing of James Joyce, alongside the works of artists Dora García, Bbeyond, and Anne Marie Dillon, among many others, to unravel how streets have been hugely contested spaces throughout history, arenas where hierarchies of power and class are played out, and yet at the same time, also offer new, radical uses for performance, activism, art, conviviality, and more.

This essay is then followed by *DAZZELGRAM a conversation about walking and leaking,* produced by The Dazzle Club. This piece is a long-form conversation which offers an original and nuanced rumination on data flows, bodies, leaking, and the sense of being watched versus being seen in public, and that looks at the opportunities and challenges posed by surveillance infrastructure. Next is the essay *Sound and the Politics of Public Space* by Rahma Khazam, a text that looks back in order to look forward. In this essay, Rahma revisits three sound art pieces that she has written about at different points throughout her career, to reflect upon what these works and their contexts can continue to tell us now about public space and its surrounding politics. The section concludes with *Does a home have an owner?*, a combined written and visual contribution from Elia Castino. In it, Elia documents his time between homes in Amsterdam, and how this experience changed his perceptions towards the public and private, especially in relation to possessions, ownership, belonging, and the city as an expanded home that offers alternative meanings for what home, place and public space can be.

The next section that follows is The Politics of Access, which focuses on questions of who is able to be a witness in public space, who is welcomed, and who is not. *L as in Walking* by Pauline Agustoni begins this section with a short introductory essay, followed with a selection of interview transcripts, that focus on the experience of lesbian and trans women, and nonbinary people living in Berlin. In the interviews, each speaker chooses a public space that holds resonance and meaning to them, walking Pauline, and, in turn, us, through these spaces with their charged descriptions. Collectively the interviews explore how those who are excluded from public space are often also excluded from public history and public memory. This is followed by Kevin Gotkin's essay *Stair Worship: Heatherwick's Vessel* originally published in The Avery Review in 2019, which investigates the politics surrounding the Vessel, a basket-like structure that opened in Hudson Yards, New York in 2019. The Vessel is made of 154 interconnected stairways and was created by designer Thomas Heatherwick. Despite a production budget nearing $150 million, the elevator that offers the only alternative to the stairways is not an equitable means to experience the structure. Kevin describes in the essay how, from its inception, the Vessel has centered the experience of climbing stairs, and, in doing so, has made itself not only inaccessible and ableist in its form, but totally unrepresentative of the society it claims to mirror through its design and function. The essay is coupled with a conversation between Kevin Gotkin and Shannon Finnegan, in which they revisit Kevin's article, alongside Shannon's *Anti-Stairs Club Lounge at the Vessel* project, where fifty disabled and non-disabled people gathered to protest at the Vessel shortly after its public opening. The conversation can be read both as an addendum to Kevin's original *Stair Worship* essay, as well as a standalone dialogue on the place the Vessel continues to hold societally and politically today. The final contribution to this section is the essay *Een huis in Indië / A house in the Dutch East Indies*, by Paoletta Holst, a text that works on multiple levels. It is at once a retelling of a conversation and experience Paoletta had that deeply, and lastingly affected her and her research, as well as a powerful documentation, and anecdotal exploration into the architectural and societal segregation that was present in Semarang, Indonesia, under Dutch colonial rule.

Then, much as this publication begins with the body, it ends with the body, with the final section The Body as Witness. This section hones in on our bodily experiences within cities and public space, and focuses on memory, bodily witnessing, sensory experience, and the act of walking and movement as a lubricant for the body, the senses, and the mind. Soeria van den Wijngaard's essay *Listen to the sensitive, they are the future* begins this section, and revisits the topic of sound once again, though this time to explore how sound and art can expand our emotional depths, and interpersonal relations. In her essay, Soeria draws from the work of Pauline Oliveros and Hanzi Freinacht, as well as her own practice, to look at the roles sound and listening play in influencing how we relate to one another, as well as our bodies, senses, environments, and ideas of place and space, and how we can become active witnesses to produce a more just and sustainable world. This is followed by Alessandro Marchi's essay *A Prequel to Critical Walks,* which acts as a meditation on his changing relationship with walking throughout his life. Especially focussing on how this relationship has impacted him physically, mentally, and has formed a practical and philosophical basis for his artistic practice. Next, Jeannette Petrik's contribution *Realm,* is a continuation from their textual work presented during the *Rights of Way* exhibition, which resulted from a short-term residency completed at Onomatopee in the summer of 2020. In *Realm – or, Observing the Melting of a Brain,* Jeannette dedicates their attention to the street of Lucas Gasselstraat, Eindhoven, the street where Onomatopee currently resides, to fully engage their senses, thoughts, experiences, and distractions whilst wandering up and down the street. In the text, this experience is translated into a series of fragmented observations that together form a meditative narrative that explores the many different meanings place and space can take on for us, and the associations and memories it can conjure. Corinne Heyrman's text *Blokje Om* follows. This is a two-part contribution, where the first part takes the form of a series of expanded fragments, memories and tableaux vivants that present themselves to Corinne over the course of a "discovery walk". This is coupled with the transcript of an interview Corinne conducted with Corinne, Inge and Mieke, all of whom are no longer walking, on their renewed relationship with movement and space. The section, and publication, end with a speculative, fictional piece written by Annee Grøtte Viken. The story takes our minds and bodies deep into the depths of the sea, exploring the importance of the ocean on our future cities and spaces, and therefore, on our bodies and selves.

From these short abstracts alone, the assemblage of different disciplines, backgrounds, interests, and ideas that have been brought together in this publication is easy to discern. The wide range of authors selected for this publication has very much been a purposeful endeavour. As public space is such a multi-faceted topic of study, it was crucial that this be reflected in the words of those who were invited to respond to, and explore this topic further. To then, hopefully, inspire others to do so in turn. The journey from conception to execution of this project, exhibition, and publication, has been, at times, difficult and tumultuous, and at others revealing and inspiring due to different local and global events that have caused disruption and delay, or an inability to communicate, meet, or exchange as planned. Yet this has by no means sat unnoticed in the background. Instead, these experiences have informed and enriched the project in its entirety. It has been a pleasure and privilege to work alongside so many amazing minds throughout this project, and I hope the words and works presented on these following pages will continue to compel and provoke.

I wish you an insightful, and inspiring reading experience, that not only immerses the mind and thoughts, but the body too.

Amy Gowen
September 2021

The Evolution

of Public Space

A Shout in the Street:

Some artists' dialectical theory of urbanism

CHRISTA-MARIA LERM HAYES

As much as city space has been constructed to suit the needs and wishes of its publics—albeit mostly privileged, dominant publics—it can just as much be imagined and counter-constructed to further other, improvised aims, struggles and methods of community-forming. Artists and other creative city-dwellers have been pivotal in envisioning other uses for space, as well as creating alternative modes of value and focus points. Such instances often emphasise areas of process, micro history and other-than-capitalist living and aphoristic format, over more stable, linear narratives. When Walter Benjamin began writing about the *flâneur*, asserting his individuality onto Paris' commodified spaces as transformed by the city's Hauss-mannisation (street-widening), he maintained the certainty of being someone who could command space, who would be seen and listened to. The world was for him, and those of his kind, educated, white, young and male, at the beginning of the twen-tieth century.

When he no longer belonged to this dominant group and had to flee those who sought to endanger his life on account of his being Jewish and harbouring other-than-Fascist thought during the Second World War, he wrote differently. Benjamin's *Passagen-Werk*, or *Arcades Project*, began in 1927 and remained unfinished at the time of his suicide on his flight from the approaching German army in 1940. The work departs from an investigation of the roved commercial spaces of the *flâneurs*, the Parisian *passages*, a space where economics, history, literature and art intersect. But the book, or better, the compilation of quotes and aphorisms, with additional notes and a system of visual cross-referencing, acts instead as an accumulation of voices, a collection of citations that conjure other authors, other presences and—most importantly—notable absences. The *Passagen-Werk*[1] is a collective enunciation, immediately political, even if not directly so. Its contents are "deterritorialised", removed from the centre of power, or, as Gilles Deleuze and Fèlix Guattari would call it, "minor literature". The absence ultimately concerns the author / compiler, Benjamin, and through the texts he allows for his voice to retreat. At a time when he could no longer safely be heard or seen, his long standing endorsement of directly political art channelled through broad distribution is apparent through the selected voices of the other authors presen-ted in the collection, as well as his desire to continue scholarly work, and to nurture analysis and stewardship over the voices of others, even when (or because) academic institutions and libraries were no longer a second home, and the refugee's job of daily survival consumed more and more of his time.

This absence, by extension, equally concerns all of those who were "collected", in order to be put on trains to extermination camps, or those who were hidden in the houses of German-occupied France. Old houses and windy streets lent themselves better to hiding, to finding a "shell" the size of one's body to retreat into when the SS stood in front of the door. The *Passagen-Werk*, I therefore claim, despite the canonicity of many of the authors quoted, is an intellectual project of the multitude,[2] claiming the creativity of "street culture"[3] even despite—and within—the regulatory uniformity of capitalist urbanism.

In this way, Benjamin developed what Joseph D. Lewandowski calls a dialectical theory of urbanism:

> [...] for Benjamin street culture is both an embedded socio-cultural art and a profoundly situated political practice. Such an insight is the very hallmark of Benjamin's dialectical theory of urbanism. [...] Benjamin makes explicit the context-transforming potential of the improvisational actions empirically enabled by such locations: streets provide, quite literally, the material resources for shared ways of dwelling and struggling.[4]

It was necessary for Benjamin to believe, of course, that there would continue to be others among those who could still walk the streets, who would be willing to shelter those who couldn't and improvise to make the communal "context-transforming" struggle successful. Yet for him, that success came too late.

What applied to Europe in the late 1930s can be considered transferable. Isabel Wilkerson tells us that from the USA to India, to Nazi Germany, a similar pattern of exclusion and oppression can be seen via the concept of caste.[5] Streets do not belong to subordinate members of society, still impacted by the effects of caste thinking. This has been witnessed throughout history: when one has to carry a branch of thorns to erase one's footsteps, lest a Brahman would be offended at an "Untouchable" having stepped on the same spot of ground in the street; when a descendant of an enslaved person has to cross the street to leave the footpath available for the white person claiming to own it, despite the country's Constitution claiming equal rights; or for the Jew, whose Star of David badge signalled sub-human status and impending death, despite (or because of) high academic or other achievement. Wilkerson develops that social relations built on the delusion (Benjamin's word would have been *phantasmagoria*) of caste have damaging effects for whole societies, not just victims and their heirs. City space shows how societies either adhere to these damaging feelings of superiority by erecting statues of perpetrators, or insist on them continuing to stand, performatively, to exercise violence by still commanding space. On the other hand, Wilkerson also uses public space to show how caste thinking can be overcome. Peter Eisenman's monument to the victims of the Holocaust in Berlin is one strand to her argument, and the other is the carpark near it: without plaque, covering over Adolf Hitler's bunker and site of death.[6]

Walter Benjamin's Paris could continue to serve this short essay as a focal point, especially by referring to the Situationist International[7] and *banlieu* inhabitants who have found their living spaces erased from some city maps, or by linking him to the *gillets jaunes* reclaiming the city, but an experience of space is always personal—and my personal history takes me to Ireland. I will therefore turn to a contemporary of the *Passagen-Werk*, James Joyce's *Finnegans Wake* from 1939,[8] a multi-lingual and non-linear account that was similarly constructed with visual clues ("sigla") as structural devices.[9] It is an epos of not-so privileged people in Dublin, which to a certain extent continues its predecessor *Ulysses*, 1922.[10] The "novel" is split into 18 episodes that could possibly be read as the story of two *flâneurs*,[11] Leopold Bloom and Stephen Dedalus, who are roaming the city as decidedly anti-heroic characters. Both books Joyce wrote as an emigrant, outside his native, longed-for city, which, in writing, he came to "own" in other than standard monetary ways. The books have thus the distinct advantage of not fitting any dominant conceptualisation of city and national space. Joyce subverted both colonial and Celtic nationalist reimaginings of his home, but, with his loving attention to "normal people", also steered clear of what the rising Eastern Bloc embraced; his characters were not normative workers either. That the characters are not well-functioning capitalists is a matter of course and despite the present-day commercialised frolicking in period costume along Dublin streets on 16 June, what Joyce's books, especially *Finnegans Wake*, are essentially asking of its readers is to find as many differently socialised people and engage in shared meaning-making with them. Essentially, to build reading groups.[12]

Dora García has taken Joyce's works into art and city spaces in this spirit. Her delegated performances in the streets, one of which is Muenster, has left passers-by uncertain as to whether they had just engaged in a pleasant exchange with a beggar, or whether they had become part of an artwork. This is a kind of attention to life that is re-calibrated by art and that has become a "territory" for artists to explore, particularly artists with a formative experience of reading Joyce. One of these artists was Joseph Beuys. Beuys had politicians in Germany quite paranoid, they knew they had to engage with this world-famous artist, but did not want to be made part of his artworks. His strategies, at times, took the fairly spectacular form of sit-ins at the Dusseldorf Academy, from which Professor Beuys was dismissed for accepting anyone who wanted to study with him into his class. In the Northern Ireland of the "Troubles," in 1974, he intervened by making friends and establishing an educational network, the Free International University for Interdisciplinary Research.[13] 1972 had seen Bloody Sunday in Derry, where the British Army shot 13 unarmed civilians demonstrating for Civil Rights, including the right to education. The Protestant / Loyalist government, in the hope of cementing caste privilege, had decided to establish a campus at the local university in a rural Protestant area, rather than in the historic city of Londonderry / Derry, with a Catholic / Republican majority. Beuys, by establishing alternative institutions (he paid the initial rent for a performance and exhibition space for an artists' collective called Art and Research Exchange) and using the local museum for a 3 ½ hour lecture and discussion, accounted for the fact that city streets were dangerous places, but communication had to happen to overcome divisions.

The local performance art collective, Bbeyond, with direct links to the people who had worked with Beuys in the 1970s, have now, for more than 15 years performed together in public space at a specific time each month. Holding space, doing "strange" things in public, taking a durational approach belongs, I would argue, to those strategies that do not let the always contested public sphere be "owned" by divisive political forces. In the *Rights of Way* exhibition, comparable and locally fine-tuned work is to be found in the contribution by The Dazzle Club, who adopt CV Dazzle face paint before enacting collective silent walks across key public and privately owned public spaces across London; or the work of Pauline Agustoni who collects oral testimony from interviewees who perform long walks whilst they talk, to tell both an individual and collective story of the public presence of lesbian women in public space.

"A Shout in the Street" was the Northern Irish curator Declan McGonagle's title for his instalment in a series of Collective Histories of Northern Irish Art at Golden Thread Gallery in Belfast. It is a quote from James Joyce that reflects how Stephen Dedalus, the alter ego of the younger writer, had defined God, knowing that the Catholic hegemony at the time would not have agreed. McGonagle, speaking in the context of his exhibition, Belfast 2008, reflected on the responsibility people felt in calling anyone to gather and demonstrate in the streets despite loss of life being a distinct possibility. Finding other forms of address, of constructing alternative civic and urban realities, while not just occupying space, may also be a sign of caring and art with that track record has something to teach to all those facing similar situations, due to Covid-19 and its succession of lockdowns. Starting with small groups: reading groups, educational initiatives, small and durational performance artworks, instead of politically charged mass meeting and "holding" space—this may be all that can be done in certain situations, and it is not insignificant. Rethinking the city through walks in brown, "unused" sites, singing together (at a distance), gathering the multitude's knowledge of a given space through hand-drawn maps, all values, raises awareness and exercises different ways of thinking. The hand-drawn map project, combined with gathering nicknames of places and walks, is an example the work of Aisling O'Beirn's in Belfast.[14]

There is also the work of Anne Marie Dillon who tested the publicness of space by letting her horse graze in Belfast's city centre: the space between court buildings that until only recently had been surveyed by a Police watchtower was less of a problem than the apparently public but, as it turned out, privately owned space outside the Waterfront Hall, a conference and concert venue with a deceptively open security glass façade just like the adjacent office buildings.[15] What can, it seems from these cases, help to speak of the love of a contested city is the gathering of local knowledge, of micro-history and small idiosyncrasies; archival projects, both in the sense of using existing archives and securing oral histories by gathering evidence of empathic human actions. Collecting micro-histories in that vein may take

Image Credit: Aisling O'Beirn, *Some Things About Belfast*, in Space Shuttle, Six Projects of Urban Creativity and Inclusion, Mission Three: North Street / Waring Street (Belfast)', curated by PS², 20 September—5 October 2006

place in instances such as the work of Seamus Harahan, who has for years lived in Belfast's student area, rife with violence and neglect. He videoed from his window ordinary peoples' slightly extraordinary lives, instances of "recreational rioting", or a 15-minute attempt at parking a small car. Such artworks might highlight, analyse and historicize conditions, collect evidence of communities re-envisioning a dysfunctional, policed environment as their space, but they also show love: that of others and the artists' own.

Performance art can pay attention to the history of places. To the small, usually unnoticed "cracks" in the city fabric, as well as the affects embodied in the non-normative bodies of inhabitants, including what they have witnessed and the emotional labour that is necessary for survival. Sandra Johnston is a Belfast performance artist, who sensitively responds to her home city's needs.[16] She has carried out research on the potential of performance methods in relation to transitional justice. Gendered violence in Belfast has played a formative role, yet reading Joyce's writings has too. At an open window, while overhearing what ordinary people, similar to those in *Ulysses* said, Joyce had given these "shouts in the street" the status of "epiphanies", revelatory moments about life, about people in and of cities.

Art has possibilities, restricted ones, but also newly calibrated ones, especially if and when streets are not the inclusive, happy mingling spaces as which planners and politicians have wished us to view them, and as which Walter Benjamin still longed to frame them, despite all their complexities. Artists from Hitler to Constant, and members of the Situationist International, have sought to reshape our city spheres in remarkably distinctive ways. When Hitler's visions left not much more than rubble, utopian visions of car-driven lives extricated living, working and socializing spheres away from each other, while keeping property rights in place and conveniently disabling memory and mourning.[17]

The joint challenges of the Covid-19 pandemic, including ecological, human and multi-generational family needs have to now be used to re-envision the spaces for our—and the planet's—lives differently: likely with fewer airmiles, closer to home, and where neighbourly relations have changed, due to the needs to make do with what—and who—is close by under lockdown. This includes mending and helping, rather than depending on the spoils of "funshopping" (as the Dutch Prime Minister is calling it). At the time of writing this short essay, in Spring 2021, the streets now belong to delivery drivers in precarious employment, to others on the "front line", and to those without the privilege of enough space behind closed doors, or remotely accessible work. Accessing some sites through literature, such as "Benjamin's" Paris passages, might just be something, while reading in isolation, that feels like a shared experience through time and space: a joint intellectual investment that lets those with books in their hands (and time for reading) long for the meeting places that they love, and, in reading, at least affectively own.[18]

Benjamin's multi-layered exploration of the passages might also teach us more about the privilege of being on the street with others, but also about *not* being there. Such thoughts demand thoughtfully to be expanded or modified for other groups, e.g. women. What has been repressive about regarding women's "place" at home also reveals an element of privilege—and the worsening of instances of domestic abuse, along with regression concerning hard-won equalities. For many women, neither public nor private space has been, or is particularly safe, not so much a space of individuation and exciting adventure, but of harassment.[19] The scale of the effects of Covid lockdowns will only register, when streets are again "inhabitable", in the sense of the creative street culture that Walter Benjamin envisaged. Instances of absence from the streets, such as (self)protection during a pandemic, or dictatorial conditions, leaves behind silence, but possibly, hopefully, also the evidence of live-saving improvisations:

> [...] in the urban milieu it is not the idealizing, context-transcending norms of validity-claims but rather the practical, context-dependent ways of improvisational dwelling and struggling that bind social actors together. Hence the dialectic of urbanism presented in Benjamin's *Passagenwerk* is not merely a blueprint for some future project. Instead, it is a material description of the persistent power, however attenuated, of urban collectives to transform the cities they inhabit, if only one street at a time.[20]

The voices that have been silenced call for collection and scholarly or neighbourly effort, akin to the material gathered by Benjamin in *Passagen-Werk*, or an individual shout in the street. They call for collectives among residents—or among artists in an exhibition, such as *Rights of Way*. As Paoletta Holst researches and makes visible the segregational features of the Dutch colonial landscapes in Semarang, Java, Indonesia, spatial hierarchy becomes visible. Similarly, Shannon Finnegan, with their *Anti-Stairs Club Lounge*, shows who can and cannot go where in privileged Western spaces that purport to be open to all. Corinne Heyrman lends her mobility and that of the audience to those who cannot walk, while Elia Castino focuses on "rough music", i.e. banging pots and pans, as means of protest. Such histories conjure global connections and possibilities for solidarity: women in Northern Ireland during the "Troubles" used metal dust bin lids to bang on the tarmac and warn their Catholic / Republican neighbours of approaching British forces' raids. And I remember Alfredo Jaar, from Cuba, telling my Belfast students that this practice had deeply touched him, when he read about it in the newspaper. He referred to it in his early artwork: drawing bin lid-sized rings on street surfaces, claiming space for liberating causes on the other side of the world.

Artists of all forms are attentive to potential connections, to non-linear stories, to archives of multiple voices, connected micro- and macro-histories, to education, traces of trauma and expressions of love. They can forge new uses of space within, or independent of sites with specifically complex constellations of need and opportunity—and enable thoughtful re-organizations. This is what the curatorial statement to the *Rights of Way* exhibition calls a "civil choreography".

Who can or will better listen to the shouts in the street? How, where and with whom will we walk and dance?

[1]
Benjamin, Walter, *Das Passagen-Werk*, 2 volumes, Frankfurt/M.: Suhrkamp 1982.

[2]
Hardt, Michael, Antonio Negri, *Multitude: War and Democracy in the Age of Empire*, London: Penguin 2004.

[3]
Lewandowski, Joseph D. "Street Culture: The Dialectic of Urbanism in Walter Benjamin's Passagen-Werk." *Philosophy & Social Criticism*, vol. 31, no. 3, May 2005, pp. 293–308.

[4]
Ibid p.304

[5]
Wilkerson, Isabel, *Caste: The Origin of Our Discontents*, New York: Random House 2020.

[6]
ibid

[7]
McDonough, Tom (ed), *The Situationists and the City*, London: Verso 2010.

[8]
Joyce, James, *Finnegans Wake*, London: Faber & Faber (1939) 2001.

[9]
ibid

[10]
Joyce, James. *Ulysses*, London: Random House, (1922) 2001.

[11]
ibid

[12]
Lerm Hayes, Christa-Maria, "Mad, Marginal, Minor (Artistic) Research" / "De la recherce (artistique) folie, marginale et mineure", Dora García, *Mad Marginal: Cahier #4*, Chantal Pontbriand (ed). Berlin: Sternberg Press 2015, pp. 120–133, 298–312. www.sternberg-press.com/index. php?pageId=1610&bookId=504&l=en

[13]
Lerm Hayes, Christa-Maria, "Beuys's Legacy in Artist-led University Projects", *Tate Papers*, no.31, Spring 2019, https://www.tate.org.uk/research/ publications/tate-papers/31/ beuys-legacy-artist-led-university-projects, accessed 28 June 2019.

[14]
Chan, Suzanna, Christa-Maria Lerm Hayes. "The Role of Diversity in the Production and Reception of Art in Belfast: Space Shuttle." Christa-Maria Lerm Hayes, Victoria Walters (eds). *Beuysian Legacies in Ireland and Beyond: Art, Culture and Politics*. Münster, Hamburg, Berlin, Vienna, London: LIT 2011

[15]
Martin Krenn, Land's End

[16]
Johnston, Sandra. *Beyond Reasonable Doubt: An Investigation of Doubt, Risk and Testimony Through Performance Art Processes in Relation to Systems of Legal Justice.* Series: European Studies in Culture and Policy. Berlin, Münster, Vienna, Zurich, London: LIT 2014.

[17]
Mitscherlich, Alexander. *Die Unwirtlichkeit unserer Städte*, Frankfurt a. M.: Suhrkamp 1965.

[18]
Solnit discusses the link between walking and reading in Solnit, Rebecca. *Wanderlust: A History of Walking.* Chicago: University of Chicago Press, 2001.

[19]
Women and Equalities Committee, House of Commons, "What Is the Nature of the Problem? Sexual Harassment of Women and Girls in Public Places" *UK Parliament Publications*, publications.parliament.uk/pa/ cm201719/cmselect/cmwomeq/701/ 70105.htm. This source was brought to my attention by the curator of the exhibition *Rights of Way*, Amy Gowen.

[20]
Lewandowski, Joseph D. "Street Culture: The Dialectic of Urbanism in Walter Benjamin's Passagen-Werk." *Philosophy & Social Criticism*, vol. 31, no. 3, May 2005, pp. 305

Bibliography

Benjamin, Walter, Das Passagen-Werk, 2 volumes, Frankfurt/M.: Suhrkamp 1982.

Chan, Suzanna, Christa-Maria Lerm Hayes. "The Role of Diversity in the Production and Reception of Art in Belfast: Space Shuttle." Christa-Maria Lerm Hayes, Victoria Walters (eds). Beuysian Legacies in Ireland and Beyond: Art, Culture and Politics. Münster, Hamburg, Berlin, Vienna, London: LIT 2011

Hardt, Michael, Antonio Negri, Multitude: War and Democracy in the Age of Empire, London: Penguin 2004.

Christa-Maria Lerm Hayes, Joyce in Art: Visual Art Inspired by James Joyce. Foreword: Fritz Senn, envoi: James Elkins, design: Ecke Bonk. The Lilliput Press Dublin 2004. A pdf is available at: http://synergeticalab.com/archive.html

Johnston, Sandra. Beyond Reasonable Doubt: An Investigation of Doubt, Risk and Testimony Through Performance Art Processes in Relation to Systems of Legal Justice. Series: European Studies in Culture and Policy. Berlin, Münster, Vienna, Zurich, London: LIT 2014.

Joyce, James, Finnegans Wake, London: Faber & Faber (1939) 2001.

Joyce, James. Ulysses, London: Random House, (1922) 2001.

Lerm Hayes, Christa-Maria, "Beuys's Legacy in Artist-led University Projects", Tate Papers, no.31, Spring 2019, https://www.tate.org.uk/research/publications/tate-papers/31/beuys-legacy-artist-led-university-projects, accessed 28 June 2019.

Lerm Hayes, Christa-Maria, "Mad, Marginal, Minor (Artistic) Research" / "De la recherche (artistique) folie, marginale et mineure", Dora García, Mad Marginal: Cahier #4, Chantal Pontbriand (ed). Berlin: Sternberg Press 2015, pp. 120–133, 298–312. www.sternberg-press.com/index.php?pageId=1610&bookId=504&l=en

Lerm Hayes, Christa-Maria, Victoria Walters (eds). Beuysian Legacies in Ireland and Beyond: Art, Culture and Politics. Münster, Hamburg, Berlin, Vienna, London: LIT 2011.

Lewandowski, Joseph D. "Street Culture: The Dialectic of Urbanism in Walter Benjamin's Passagen-Werk." Philosophy & Social Criticism, vol. 31, no. 3, May 2005, pp. 293–308.

McDonough, Tom (ed), The Situationists and the City, London: Verso 2010.

Mitscherlich, Alexander. Die Unwirtlichkeit unserer Städte, Frankfurt a. M.: Suhrkamp 1965.

Solnit, Rebecca. Wanderlust: A History of Walking. Chicago: University of Chicago Press, 2001.

Wilkerson, Isabel, Caste: The Origin of Our Discontents, New York: Random House 2020.

Women and Equalities Committee, House of Commons, "What Is the Nature of the Problem? Sexual Harassment of Women and Girls in Public Places" UK Parliament Publications, publications.parliament.uk/pa/cm201719/cmselect/cmwomeq/701/70105.htm.

Declan McGonagle, A Shout in the Street: Collective Histories of Nothern Irish Art, Sarah McAvera (ed), Belfast: Golden Thread Gallery 2008.

DAZZLEGRAM

a conversation about leaking and walking

THE DAZZLE CLUB

TRANSCRIPTION KEYWORDS
leaking, data, walk, seeing, feeling, people, held, cameras, scraping, describe, talking, dazzle, leader, human, information, movement, watching, listening, choreography, squeezing.

I want to tell you about my dream.

I've been thinking about data and where it is, and whether there can be two kinds. A data of being watched, made up of ones and zeros—I don't really understand what that looks like, but I know it's harvested and scraped. It's in big servers that use loads of energy and it's used for things like watchlists. It's biased and problematic. How can we describe its stuckness? It's fixed. It's trained to only see certain things.

So that's the data of watching.

Then there's the data of seeing. When my neighbour said, 'I'm feeling seen', I understood how being seen feels different. Feeling seen. Seeing. What does that kind of data look like? Where does it get stored? I guess it's in our bodies, and if not, it's in someone else's body. It's of the body and within the body, which is where surveillance terms like scraping and leaking and flowing feel relevant.

So, I was thinking about my dream last night. I was swimming and so clearly sensed the water on the back of my hand as my arm slid through its surface—my body as a solid, moving through this thick liquid. And so, when then thinking about data, I wondered whether 'being seen' is more like that fluid stuff, if it is more like how that water felt when my arm slipped through it. Is that kind of data always flowing? Can we describe it in that way? It slides off us. And then it ripples away to touch something else?

Is it somewhere in the sliding and the slipping that we are seen? Is seeing being held, like the water holds us?

Touch.

I'm interested in this kind of floppy, free data, the 'being seen' data. As you described—it is holding, it is supporting.

Or is holding ourselves, and our data, something we do to prevent being watched? Do we feel we have to adapt our behaviours—some of us more than others—due to the bias of algorithms? Does this then connect to discussions about what feeling free might be like in public space?

Is that 'being seen' data therefore a contradiction or a healthy ecology?

A collective holding of ourselves and each other could take place by acting freely wherever we are in the city, rather than the other way around. Are we waiting to be free, instead of making it happen?

So, you're making a distinction between two types of data—human data, and the machine data that is seeing us.

We can't see either type of data. It's all invisible.

When we walk in the city and feel watched, we can feel it. And we, well I anyway, often feel angry or claustrophobic. My neighbour standing on the doorstep describing a feeling of being seen—we don't have a quantifying system for that do we? If we are calling it data, is the first step towards knowing that data trying to describe how it feels? Is that what we have been finding out through dazzle walking[1]—how this human data feels? I'm just beginning to think that if we're proposing 'being seen', not being watched, how can we begin to describe what 'being seen' is?

I think we experience 'being seen' as a collective when we're moving together. Those cameras are all there, and there's a kind of alarm and a sense of awareness, and there's also this incredible sense of community and pleasure. Joyfulness.

Control.

The security polemic argues these infrastructures of surveillance provide comfort and security—that we are made safe because of these things. It's interesting trying to differentiate between machine and human data and realising that humans created those very infrastructures anyway. We need a new way of talking about being held, feeling secure and safe.

Have we been persuaded to believe that we are being held?
Are we being made safe through all this watching? In some way
we're saying 'no, that's not being held, that's being controlled'.
And yes, maybe sometimes the watching has stopped something
happening or found a killer or a rapist, however we know that
mostly what it does is something else—or nothing at all. Relent-
less capturing.

I realise there's a danger of a binary here, saying that 'this' is on
this side, and 'this' is on that. Possibly that's what we are seeking
through making a dazzlegram,[2] a way of expressing where
effects/benefits/outcomes/intrusions are overlapping? And when
they are needing to be pulled apart?

We think about hardware, the infrastructures that you spoke of,
as fixed and tough. And yet the materiality of the electricity,
even the cabling itself, is dynamic. The movement of information
is fluid. Is the hardware emphasised because its masculinity
appears to offer reliability—something visible for us to compre-
hend?

There is great movement. Or is it speed, not movement? Because
of the power of the technology. Like fibre. The language around
the fibre optic is 'hyper fast'. Isn't it that it can get from here
to the satellite, before I've even pointed my finger. I don't know
how I didn't quite get a sense of that before. But there's something
about the speed and the scale of it now—the power—that has
sharpened my understanding.

Yes, it's instantaneous—the goal is for it to be instantaneous,
total efficiency.

And, the error, the lag, is important. If there are errors in the
technology, that is the window of opportunity where a crime can
take place, where a crime could happen.

I'm thinking about your tutor[3] not really understanding your
interest in the lag and the space of freedom that it offers. It's about
those moments of invisibility.

And last week, another tutor used the word 'trudging' about the
way that I walk across the screen, and how that's a quality

that you might not consider when thinking about the digital experience. I think that's what's curious about the way we talk about data and explore what these systems are in an organic and embodied way.

Skin.

Is 'total efficiency' military terminology? We see more and more how this kind of vocabulary is being used in medical language—'fighting covid', the 'battle against', 'fighters', 'soldiering on', 'the siege', 'the enemy within'.

Leaking, scraping, collecting—the words are used to describe collecting and testing of bodily fluids and samples, as well as the data that we emit, or give off. There is a feeling that people in public space are not really aware of this data that we're giving off. Would anything change if we were? But also, by giving off this data, it can be used in the future. We're giving more information for people to understand ourselves, potentially better.

'Leaking' is also curious because it belongs so aptly to the 'being seen' world. When you slip up emotionally, it's a vulnerability. And it's really where we start being human. But at the same time, the idea that we are leaking data... are we instead being harvested, extracted?

Where is that from? The idea of leaking is that through our use of social media or through our daily life, in a normal journey to work, we're getting a certain amount of information scraped from us by something. Is this something that we're doing willingly? Or is it something that we're doing unconsciously?

Behavioural surplus[4] is an excess that we're producing—there's an excess of information with everything that we do both online and IRL. And maybe that's where the leaking comes from in my mind.

I have to take it right back to the body, because women's bodies leak all sorts of stuff all the time, conventionally perceived as waste or mess. What if our menstrual leaks are evidence of empowering abundance, flipping the leaking from a patriarchal language of loss and weakness.

If we can't trust them, [5] we have to control them.

Our existence as a human is that we are constantly leaking information. We are in an unprecedented time, where we are living
within a psychological operation by Big Tech. Young people
are being trained to think that self-expression, or our identity as
a person, is having an Instagram profile, a Facebook profile,
and 'living' means interacting with other people through these
channels. We are expected to upload so much information,
which is monetised and that we then live within. We're going to
see the effect of this in decades to come—how identity and
self-expression has been warped and exploited. It's that leaking
that we are being persuaded to do, in several decades time,
we will look at ourselves and wonder what happened.

Leaking your existence.

I'm trying to answer a question about which data is important.
Annoyingly, I think a lot of people probably including myself,
would argue that most data could be important in some way because of how we might interpret this data in the future. Maybe
that's where the barrier hits, or the argument starts between the
collection, the processing, and the scraping of all that data?
We're forever trying to find reasons as to why facial recognition
could be a good thing. And there are of course positives in all
these things. It's just this very frustrating cycle when information
is then used to capitalise on something.

I like the idea of 'good things' as well. Maybe some of the data that
is being collected, I guess the medical application of facial
recognition is a good example of this, might be useful later. We
don't know what data might be being collected now, on our
bodies, that might later become beneficial.

Currently facial recognition algorithms are biased, systemically
racist, because this is how they have been made. Those
machines were trained. But the camera isn't the bit that has been
trained to be racist. It's the algorithm.

If we want to devise security which is about care and not watching, which is about seeing and not watching, then might
tech collect the same data but do something different with it?

Are there other processes of watching as well? You might include for example the security guards who are using the systems and who are trained to use them in a certain way. Or the person who's ordered the cameras to be put on that wall through the procurement processes that are established around an ideology of control. So it's behavioural as well. Whether it's a human or machine, it's in the software inside, not the hardware.

Is it not both the software and hardware design because the manufacture and evaluation of hardware is made through a patriarchal framework, versus the concepts of care which are drawn from the norms of femininity? What could a feminist infrastructure of seeing be?

Surface.

Do we want to talk about the act of walking in itself?

Dazzle walking is a very specific experience, a defiant walking together, walking with others.

Silent exchange.

It's also not about being silent, is it? It's about listening. To listen to the city. Rather than ask people to be silent, we ask people to listen. I am intrigued by trying to describe it more accurately. To find our words for what happens—if there are words.

But isn't it also about that act of insistence? Which I think is resistance, which is saying we need to really see the cameras. It's an invitation. We're inviting people to see the cameras with their own bodies. Then it is possible to see them with our whole bodies, not just a rational mind.

I feel like there's something in the invitation of the walk that creates a different sort of attention. We are inviting you to listen instead of talk, and that shifts the attention that we might otherwise place elsewhere.

Maybe it's holding a different sort of attention around structures of surveillance that normally we might not give our attention to.

When I'm leading the walk, there are things happening that feel like they have kind of been staged. It's incredible how that kind of alertness to what's going on, to the present moment, in a public space, suddenly hits. It's like, oh, that person must have been placed right there to make that noise or do that thing as the line walks by?

I remember that day where we walked up the steps of Granary Square. We became part of the sunset spectacle. In a way, we needed to walk there. But also, it's been a real pleasure walking in the places that haven't yet been consumed or commodified. One of the things I like about the Dazzle Walk is this insistence that it keep exploring, that it keeps going to new places.

The open invitation means it's not always the same people attending. And therefore, there's a new exchange that happens between the people that are on the walk, and through the discussion we have afterwards.

Walkers are both from that place and new to that place, bringing different perspectives.

The walks are small things. An intimate group setting. So, through the conversations there is a getting to know not just the place but each other. And then we go off into the night.

There's also something important in how we locate ourselves at the starting point and paint up together. That is an essential part of the choreography, bringing walkers out of the passivity of being a person in public space. The process of applying the face paint makes us hyper-visible.

When we're painting up together, we're bodies in a space. We are stationary in one place. When we set off there is this flow of us moving to reach the end point and gather again.

There's a flow of us in a line of following.

It's funny, we're never expecting people to walk in a line, but nine times out of ten it happens.

Is that because of how we move about the city—or more specifically London? I get frustrated by people that fill up the whole pavement. This kind of squeezing through the city keeps the flow.

Stationary, fluid, stationary. The settled gathering at the beginning and the end. And then this squeeze through the fluid.

We are a line of information. Or data. We're data. We're just a bit of data moving through the city.

Afterwards.

A week after this conversation, London Met trawled through CCTV footage from buses and front doors to find a woman who had disappeared. And the rest of us were told to stay indoors to keep safe.

The cameras tragically didn't find a woman walking home safe. And her violent death has focused our minds once again on public space.

The strategy—to implant plain clothes police officers in night clubs to watch over us, to install CCTV cameras in alleyways, dissolves the last of our hidden public spaces to the watchful eye of Big Tech and proliferates this infringement of watching—not in the caring 'feeling seen' seeing—but in the watching way.

Through this conversation, we found that the dazzlegram is a conversation, not a little diagram.

The dazzlegram is the discussion before and after the walking, it is the stationary space where these things can land, a memoir, a settling.

We strive to continue—we thought it would be for two years, but the insistence is to keep walking together. There's more to know, and we make ourselves available to that knowing with our bodies. To walk without fail. Despite a year of walking through some form of restriction, we kept going.

We will continue to occupy the lag, not the total efficiency, so that in the aesthetic of complexity and blur we find a usefulness, a possibility, for a future kind of surveillance.

We keep believing in a security of care.
Anna Hart, Evie Price, Emily Roderick, Georgina Rowlands, The Dazzle Club

April 2021

[1]
Since August 2019, The Dazzle Club
has organised a Dazzle Walk for every
third Thursday of the month—a choreo-
graphed silent walk where participants
wear *CV Dazzle*, a concept designed
by Adam Harvey in 2010 to confuse
face detection algorithms.

[2]
Dazzlegram is an idea-in-progress, a
potential tool for communicating our
surveillance research.

[3]
EP is currently a 3rd year BAFA student
at Central Saint Martins, whose current
work scrutinises the new publicness
of our private spaces through the
increased use of video conferencing
software during the pandemic.

[4]
Shoshana Zuboff coined 'behavioral
surplus' to describe the leftovers after
commercial use of our extracted data
to improve products or services.

[5]
Was our 'them' here referring to those
who believe that to collect data is to
keep us safe, to control space/body/
future? Or it is a big brother voice,
speaking about 'them'—the free
citizen, the women, the marginalised.

49

Sound and the politics of Public Space

RAHMA KHAZAM

What if we were to consider public space in terms of sound rather than vision? Can sound be a marker of urban transformation, in the same way as visual evidence? Can sound shed light on tensions in public space? This essay will look at the work of three artists who have been exploring these questions for nearly two decades. Rather than looking at their current output, it will focus on pieces dating back ten or more years. Such works have the advantage of demonstrating that the use of sound to engage with political, social, and environmental tensions is by no means a new development, but a long-term artistic endeavour that can mirror, track, and even foreshadow the evolution of public space.

Christina Kubisch's 'Electrical Walks', for example, is an ongoing project for groups of walkers, the first iteration of which took place in Cologne in 2004 and was followed by further iterations taking place all over the world, from Cracow to Lagos, Moscow to Hong Kong. Exploring the spread of electromagnetic fields in urban areas, the walks allow visitors to access the sounds of wireless communication equipment, radar systems, anti-theft security devices, cell phones, computers, and streetcar cables. They can also experience the varying volumes and timbres of these sounds, some of which are common to all cities, while others can only be discerned in a particular place. Wearing specially designed wireless headphones, participants hear rhythmic beats, lengthy drones, eerie wails, or distant signals as they approach or pass by neon signs, surveillance cameras or lighting systems. The slightest movement of the head or a step or two to one side can provoke abrupt changes in the sounds, encouraging listeners to create their own choreography as they make their way around a city or town. As they do so, they 'play' the architecture, as it were, summoning sounds from within it. As the artist notes: 'The perception of everyday reality changes when one listens to the electromagnetic fields [...] Nothing looks the way it sounds. And nothing sounds the way it looks'.[1]

That these electromagnetic sounds can be extremely precise markers of urban change, is illustrated by the walk Kubisch planned for the city of Oberhausen in 2010, where a new shopping centre had been erected in an old industrial area. Here, the melodious sounds issuing from the older systems contrasted sharply with the more disjointed ones produced by the newer electromagnetic fields. As the artist herself writes, looking back on the changes that have occurred since she devised the first walks: 'There is almost no more electrical silence. Security gates that are very rhythmic are replaced more and more by new technologies with extremely loud and high continuous signals. Many "beautiful" sounds based on analogue techniques have completely disappeared. This concerns for example lighting systems, television monitors, trams. There are many more antennas and internet signals in open spaces in cities. The electromagnetic networks have become much denser, expanding quickly in African countries for example, where some time ago there was not even electricity'.[2]

By sonifying these electromagnetic fields, Kubisch not only offers access to an aspect of public space that is generally beyond bounds, but she also allows us to witness the growing presence of these hidden by-products of our industrial civilization, whose effects on our health are not yet fully known. The walks also have a more positive dimension in that they encourage participants to be more aware of, and interested in their surroundings. They connect the participants with each other and emphasize the local rather than the global, helping to make public space more welcoming and accessible.

Justin Bennett's 'Shotgun Architecture' project highlights the restrictive nature of public space. The project began in 2008, when Bennett fired a starting gun in different parts of the Zuidas, Amsterdam's business district. He recorded the impulse responses and used them to make a sound composition as well as visual renderings of the acoustic space. More than just artistic material however, the pistol shots were also a way of exploring the limits on freedom of action in public space. Although it was, and still is, legal to own or fire a starting pistol, in practice anyone doing so is more than likely to be stopped for aggressive behaviour—all the more so today, and even more so in the Zuidas, where many of the public areas are privately owned or controlled in addition to being monitored by security companies, each of which enforces its own strict rules. Bennett's project bears witness to the norms that regulated public space back then. Looking back at it today, we realize that those regulations also gestured to an incipient authoritarianism that has since become endemic in public space.

In carrying out the project, Bennett became aware of other problems arising with respect to the use of public space. The policy in the Zuidas was that new office buildings had to include public areas, yet although many such spaces were built, they remained for the most part empty and uninviting.[3] For example, one particular building designed by Toyo Ito had a public garden inside it, but the public rarely used it. As Bennett points out: 'It had [...] a sort of private feeling, like you didn't really belong there'.[4] Another building designed as a public space never even opened to the public but remained out of bounds for security reasons. Bennett's project signals the attrition of the principles at the heart of the notion of public space—an issue that has become even more acute today.

Finally, 'Shotgun Architecture' bears witness to the evolution of the cityscape. The high-rise office buildings in the midst of which it was realized, were mostly built between 1999 and 2008, and the pistol shots revealed the sonic characteristics of this newly built architecture that was so different from the 1920s and 1930s buildings that had occupied much of the area before. The project showed how architecture shapes the sounds produced within it, while also highlighting the potential violence lurking beneath even the most peaceful-looking town or city. For Bennett, all these issues are literally built into the fabric of a city, as he points out in a text relating to another work of his from the same period, the computer animation *City of Progress* (2008). Here, a single dot is seen expanding outwards into squares and rectangles, culminating in a schematic city plan. He writes: 'While drawing this city, I am considering [...] ideas of the displacement of violence, the connections between destructive and creative forces, the balance between freedom and control, [...] wondering if the public spaces around me really are public'.[5] If public space was not truly public at the time 'Shotgun Architecture' was made, it is clearly even less public today.

Brandon LaBelle's claim that 'sound may radically infringe upon public space, and challenge civic notions of an ethics of display and the rights to occupation',[6] resonates with some of Mark Bain's works. Bain's project *Action Unit: Instant Riot for Portable People* (2004), for instance, is a battery-operated sound system on wheels comprising a small bass speaker with an amplifier and two large PA horns. Presented in Istanbul at an exhibition called 'Hit & Run', the piece brought together what Bain describes as '40 minutes of rage, a collection of protests from around the world mixed to reflect conflicting opinions yet share the same anger in different languages [...] a kind of Babylonian freak out which lacked any ideological content'.[7] Bain spent two months gathering the audio extracts on the radio or internet, noting how the sounds seemed to lodge in his head and continued to resound for up to an hour after he had left the editing room. When the piece was played in public in the busy shopping street in front of the Platform gallery, it had an even more powerful effect, to the point of triggering a small riot. Referencing William Burroughs, Bain describes the sounds as 'infecting' the location where they were presented, even though they were bereft of any ideological or informational content.[8] The piece also raised important moral issues. As he writes: 'The ethics of this work could also be discussed, along with how certain sounds can affect a group psychosis'.[9]

Likewise modifying the dynamics of public space, *Acoustic Space Gun* (2004) consists of a shoulder-mounted metre-long directional microphone fitted with a parabolic sound emitter pointing in the opposite direction to the microphone.[10] The piece picked up live conversations at one end, which were then amplified and projected at the other end. By detaching the projected sounds from their source, the work altered the natural acoustics of public space to disorientating effect—people could suddenly hear their own voices issuing from another part of the space or bouncing off the front of a nearby building. Like *Action Unit: Instant Riot for Portable People*, *Acoustic Space Gun* is as topical as ever, despite having been made some fifteen years ago. In addition to exploring the psychological impact of sound and the ways in which this invisible medium can be used to modify the public's behaviour,[11] both works comment on tensions that still shape society today. The first work in particular would most probably create havoc in volatile parts of the world today, even more so than in 2004. As Bain notes, politics can be a factor in deciding how, when, where, or even whether art can be presented in public space.[12]

Sound clearly takes on a whole new dimension when exhibited in public space. As Brandon LaBelle underscores: 'To move from the space of the art gallery to the realm of public space is immediately to conjure various tensions, histories, and possibilities'.[13] The works discussed here specifically attend to the tensions, histories and possibilities that determine the evolution of public space.

[1]
Electrical Walks,
http://www.christinakubisch.de/en/
works/electrical_walks (accessed 28
November 2020).

[2]
Christina Kubisch, in an email to the
author dated 14 October 2020.

[3]
Justin Bennett in conversation with
Jesse van Winden, Radio in Between
Spaces, https://www.mixcloud.com/
Zentrum_Aktuelle_Musik/ribs09-justin-
bennett-jacob-kirkegaard/ (accessed
26 November 2020).

[4]
Justin Bennett in conversation with
Jesse van Winden.

[5]
Justin Bennett, 'City of Progress', in
The City Amplified: Justin Bennett, The
Hague, Stroom Den Haag, 2009, p.80.

[6]
 Brandon LaBelle, 'Speaking Volumes',
2006, http://www.elo-repository.org/
TIRweb/feb06/SpeakingVolumes.pdf
(accessed 28 November 2020).

[7]
Mark Bain, 'Psychosonics and the
Modulation of Public Space: On Subversive Sonic Techniques', 2005, p.6,
https://onlineopen.org/psychosonics-
and-the-modulationof-public-space
(accessed 28 November 2020).

[8]
Mark Bain, 'Psychosonics', p. 6.

[9]
Mark Bain, 'Psychosonics', p. 6.

[10]
Mark Bain, 'Psychosonics', p. 9.

[11]
Mark Bain, 'Psychosonics', p. 10.

[12]
Mark Bain, in an email to the author
dated 24 November 2020.

[13]
Brandon LaBelle, 'Speaking Volumes'.

Does a home have an owner?

ELIA CASTINO

Does a home have an owner?
Is it the one who holds its property
or
is it the inhabitant?
Is it who chose the furniture that furnishes it,
the one who cares for its spaces and does the housework,
the participants to the many dinners that animate it?
Is it
who grew up in it?
who made love in it?
who said goodbye to each other in it?
everyone whose memories are held in it?

Perhaps a home belongs to who has the key to enter it.

When I had been evicted from the 10th apartment I had lived in, I forgot to return a spare entrance door key that I had been keeping in the side pocket of my backpack.

For the following 3 months I had no permanent dwelling, and the more my idea of the conventional structure of the home evaporated, the more I experienced the city differently. I wandered far and wide through the city streets: immense hallways connecting immense rooms of an expanded home.

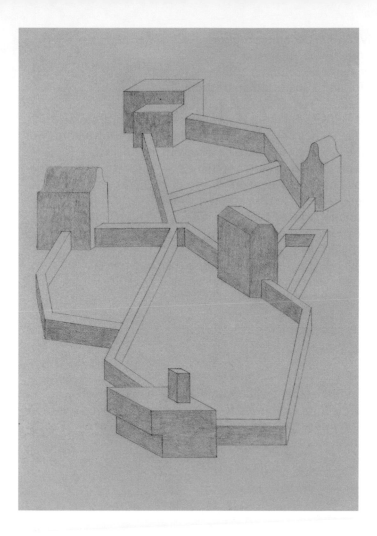

My routine became a route
to reach
my dispersed stuff:
unfolding a scattered domesticity.

The bulkiest belongings were placed in a rental storage unit.
Some clothes ended up in the locker at the shop where I worked,
some in a weekend bag I carried with me
and others in the homes of friends
whose couches I slept on
when I failed to find a short term sublet.
I managed to stay over at my 24/7 open studio at school
I ate meals at the canteen
on the go
whilst being a guest at the homes of close ones.
I did my washing at the laundromat
took showers at the swimming pool
and
hid my potted plants in flowerbeds

I wandered far and wide with that key in my pocket:
an amulet for a renewed feeling of belonging, a master key for all
the doors to make me feel the city—the home of everybody—
as mine too.

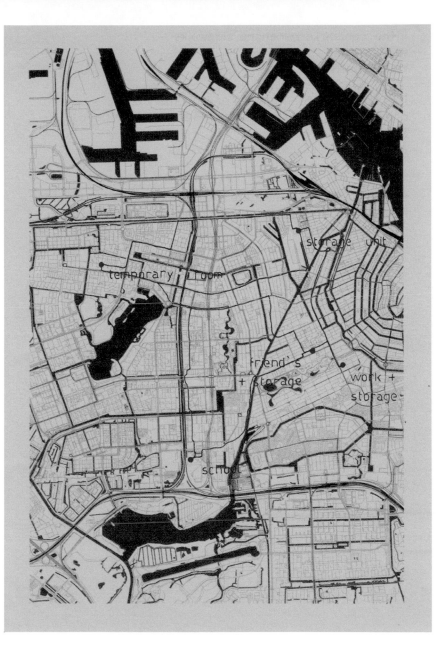

storage unit

temporary room

friend's + storage

work + storage

school

In the scenario I experienced, sidewalks
were covered
with domestic waste.

I felt the obsolescence of the conventional house
dominated by spatial typologies and commodified goods
and I envisioned
a possibility for its liberation.

Everything I needed was there and continues to be: the material
for a rearrangement in the pursuit of an essential way of living,
defining other meanings of home, place and public space.

Out of necessity
I found myself
shifting my way of inhabiting
of dealing with quotidian occurrences

rethinking
reshaping
daily life beyond its ordinary domestic shell.

Reality is illusion, so reverie is the place to inhabit.

Alaa playing his violin at my place

The Politics of

L as in Walking

PAULINE AGUSTONI

«Lesbian identity is constructed in the temporal and linguistic mobilization of space, and as we move through space we imprint utopian and dystopian moments upon urban life. Our bodies are vital signs of this temporality and intersubjective location. In an instant, a freeze-frame, a lesbian is occupying space as it occupies her.»
The lesbian flaneur, Sally Munt, 1994

When contemplating my response to the themes presented by the *Rights of Way* exhibition, I immediately thought about working with my own community. As a lesbian designer, I wanted to address the complex relationship between queer women and public space.

There is a strong link between public space and its users. They shape public space as much as it shapes them. They construct it in their image and this image in turn dictates a set of active behaviours. So what happens when stigmatized minorities evolve in public space? According to Pierre Bourdieu, «space has been, and continues to be, monopolized and controlled by particular groups of people. The very production and use of space is by and large determined by those with means, be it in terms of economic, symbolic, or political power», aka public space has historically been defined by male individuals and there has been little to no access for women and lesbians to have an influence on its structure.

How can we work against the erasure from public space—and public history—that lesbian women experience? In the shape of protests, public meetings and social gatherings, lesbian women are reclaiming a direct impact upon the spaces they evolved within. This project, *L as in Walking,* inscribes itself in this plan of action.

Lesbians often experience a double stigma—as women *and* as lesbians—which contributes to their exclusion from public space. Their rejection from certain spaces is as a result of different reasons. Firstly, the unequal economic distribution between men and women plays an important role, secondly the patriarchal norms that limit women's access to public space influences this divide and finally the dominant narrative of heteronormativity, which frames homosexuality as something abnormal that should remain invisible means that exclusion is highly present within these communities.

These elements further stimulate lesbians' removal from public space life, an effect that can be extended to their involvement in public political life. Indeed, I believe that public space and its access politics concern broader political issues. Henri Lefebvre developed a concept of social justice based on the right to access public space in the hope to transform it in his 1968 book «*Le droit à la ville*» (the right to the city). He says that «among these rights in the making [of the city] features the right to the city (not to the ancient city, but to urban life, to renewed centrality, to places of encounter and exchange, to life rhythms and time uses, enabling the full and complete usage of these moments and places, etc.). The proclamation and realization of urban life as the rule of use (of exchange and encounter disengaged from exchange value) insist on the mastery of the economic (of exchange value, the market, and commodities) and consequently is inscribed within the perspectives of the revolution under the hegemony of the working class.». David Harvey refined and developed this concept further by stating that the «rights to space are not conferred by property ownership but rather by inhabitance, a form of citizenship that is based in dwelling and acting in space.». To me, this coincides with being visible and active as lesbians in public space*. Sally Munt continues, «mobility within that space is essential, because motion continually stamps new ground with a symbol of ownership.»

L as in Walking's activist approach makes use of the methods of mobility and visibility as strategies during the interviews themselves. Microphone in hand, I direct the interviews while walking to the place the interviewee has chosen to talk about. Through talking and walking, each of the interviews further proves that despite the stigma, lesbians have grounded their lives in public space, building their own places. Whether as places they own, places they feel welcome in, places they can be themselves in and celebrate each other in. Those are the places I am interested in exploring with the project. In terms of geographical location, my community is largely based in Berlin, which allows me to quickly come in contact with many lesbians there. This is the reason why the research is grounded here. It investigates the very places that contribute to mine and my community's collective experience of the city of Berlin.

During each interview, the interviewee first expands on how the space she chose is meaningful to her as a lesbian. She then develops what this given place represents for her. Chosen spaces are as varied as a park where a couple like to take walks, the location that acted as the start of a young lesbian's first Dyke March, the route a transgender woman took when presenting female in public for the first time and a local bar where social meet-ups for lesbians are held. By linking the places to each individual, subjective experience and reading of it, and by doing it while walking, the interviewees actively make these routes, these spaces, these places their own.

As researcher Reta Ugena Whitlock says, «place is a constructed idea, like race or gender, and may thus be considered through a variety of lenses. Place is a social, cultural, geopolitical construction, as well as a geographical location.». Seeing space as a social construction is an engaging idea, because it means that we have as much impact on it as we have on ourselves. During the interviews, we are walking in the same space that we are talking about, we are *inhabiting* it. Being mobile and visible with our bodies and our voices in public space means we are leaving our mark on it.

This is crucial to my approach, as enhancing visibility of lesbians in public space—as well as in public history—is central to the project. As journalist and activist Alice Coffin rightly says, we don't fight for lesbianism to be visible to talk about our sexuality, but to reclaim a political identity. Making lesbians visible sounds like a vast program, and it is, but we are here and we have things to say, things that are valuable to tell. Our experience is special, important and yet simultaneously too obscure and unknown. It remains a mystery to most people, which further perpetuates stigma and prejudice against lesbians.

Walking while doing the interview has a second effect: it gets us into a specific rhythm for the second part of the interview, the one concerning associative words. In this part, I say a word to the interviewee and she answers with the first word that comes to her mind. It is an experiment that works towards a more spontaneous, deep and instinctive understanding of public space.

The associations are as diversified as: wall/barrier, frontier/opportunity, walking/marching, outside/freedom, territory/hostile. The words are witnesses of the special sensitivity of those who know what it feels like to belong as much as what it feels like *not* to belong.

The associative words are so striking that I decided to give them an important role in the exhibition installation and in this text.

I juxtaposed the printed words on top of the analogue photographs I took of the visited spaces. Merging with the photograph of the place, they act as a reading guide and transmit the unique perspective of a given person on a particular space. The set of words placed next to the picture confers to it a lesbian-specific context whilst simultaneously universalizing its meaning. It is an act of re-appropriation of a place's meaning whilst transferring a part of universal public space to lesbian women.

Just like the *L* in *walking*, we are there but we are not being spoken of. It is high time this changes.

Pauline Agustoni, February 2021

With warm thanks to the institutions *Spinnboden Lesbenarchiv und Bibliothek Berlin* and *IHLIA LGBTI Heritage* for their precious help with my research.

---

* It is worth mentioning that I say this in a European context. I don't undervalue the importance of invisibility in different contexts. For example, Natalie Newton rightly understands «strategic invisibility as a complex form of resistance». In her brilliant essay about the lesbian—*les* in Vietnamese—community in Saigon, she challenges «the notion that occupation of «public» space is necessarily the epitome of «queer visibility».»

SOURCES AND QUOTES:

Social space and symbolic power, Pierre Bourdieu, 1989

Invisible women in invisible places: Lesbians, lesbian bars, and the social production of people/environment relationships, Maxine Wolfe, 1992

In search of lesbian space? The experience of Manchester's gay village, Annette Pritchard, 2002

Mapping desire: geographies of sexuality, David Bell & Gill Valentine, 1995

Beyond a lesbian space? An investigation on the intergenerational discourse surrounding lesbian public social places in Amsterdam, Katherine Fobear, 2012

Entering the urban frame: Early lesbian activism and public space in Montréal, Julie A. Podmore & Line Chamberland, 2015

Space, agency and the transfiguring of lesbian/queer desire, Corie Hammers, 2009

Le droit à la ville, Henri Lefebvre, 1968

The right to the city, David Harvey, 2003

The lesbian flaneur, Sally Munt, 1994

Them ol' nasty lesbians—Queer memory, place and rural formations of lesbians, Reta Ugena Whitlock, 2009

Le génie lesbien, Alice Coffin, 2020

Contingent invisibility: Space, community and invisibility for les in Saigon, Natalie Newton, 2016

wandering
thoughtful

direction
aim

itinerant
confused

intimacy
closure

community
LGBTQ+

queer
me

crossroad
direction

locality
community

legs
running

road
freedom

openness
honesty

communication
transparency

wait
certitude

spontaneous

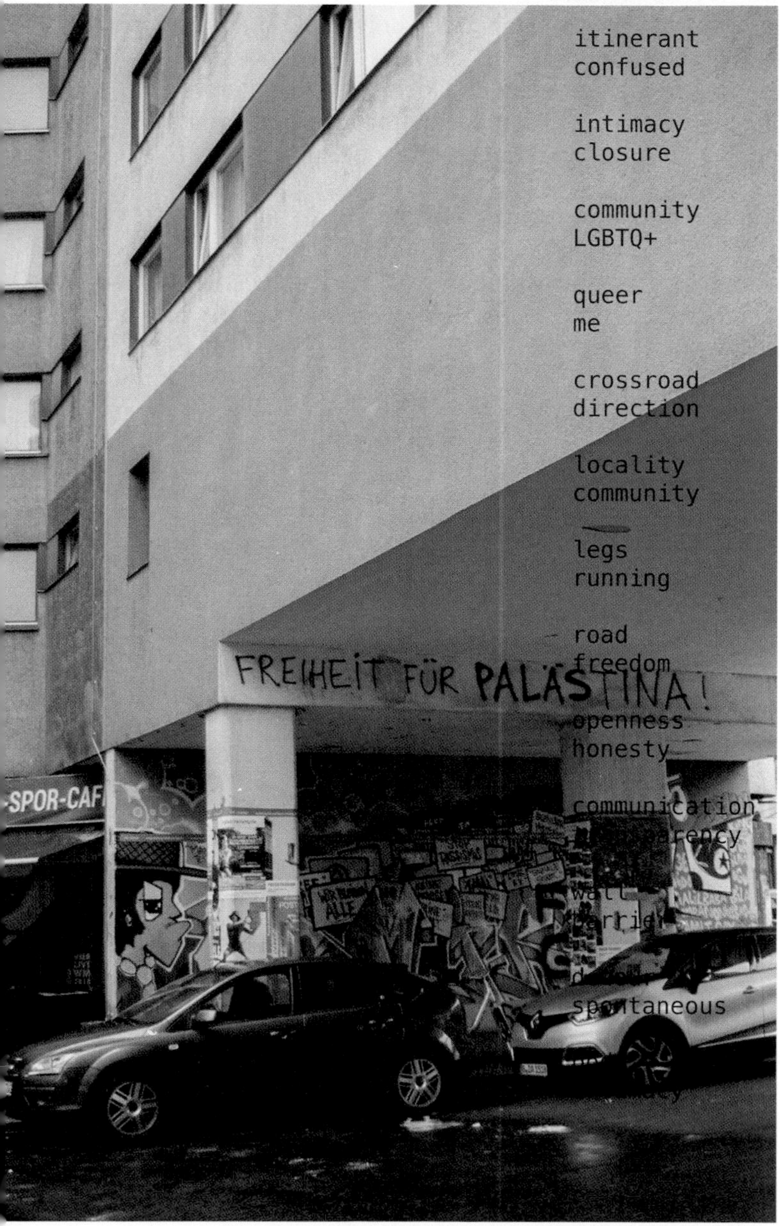

DOMINIKA

D   I want to talk about the area around Kottbusser Tor. Specifically, two places: the bar Südblock and Maybachufer, the place near the canal, where I often meet friends.

This area is very important to me for different reasons. Firstly, I connect it strongly with some of my relationships. Romances with girlfriends happened here. I kissed with a girl in front of everyone for the first time right here actually! And another one broke up with me at Maybachufer.

I also connect it with the L-Night meetups (a Berlin-based social group for queer women), which I really like to host at Südblock.

P   How do you feel in this area?

D   I feel like I can be myself here. But I always had this feeling about Berlin in general, as a city. I don't have to pretend; I don't have to prove anything to anyone. For me Berlin represents total freedom. No matter what your views are and how you act, you can just be yourself and Berlin accepts you.

P   Can you tell me more about the L-Night meetups that you organise?

D   We are a self-organized group organizing meetups for queer women or people who consider themselves as queer women. You can be a trans person, you can be a bisexual person, you can be an asexual person, as long as you perceive yourself as a queer woman you're welcome to join. It doesn't sound very inclusive at the beginning because it is for women only and not for the whole community. The reason behind it is that the queer women community is having a hard time concerning social spaces and social activities.

There are not that many bars or clubs specifically for women. It is the same with meetups and organized groups. Men have many more things being organized and it is easier for them to blend in and to find people within the community.

So, we are also doing this for the women who recently arrived in Berlin, to help them find a place for meeting people in the community easily.

I've been living here for 5 years now, and I remember that when I first moved it was hard to find other people from the queer community. I had difficulties reaching out to these people or finding a group of people. I met people through the L-Night meet-up myself so now I am very happy to help organize it. I know how important it is and how it helps people at the beginning. Then it just gets easier, you meet friends of friends, and it never ends.

P   What do you like about hosting at the bar Südblock?

D   I really like hosting the meetups here because there is a lot of space, inside as well as outside. It's also quite central so when people are coming back from work, it's kind of easy to get to from different places. It's easy to reach, you can get something to eat, it's very convenient!

P   In your opinion, how can a space, be it a neighbourhood, a bar, a café, play a role in making people feel welcome and accepted?

D   I think it's a bit of everything. Firstly, it's definitely how the place is built and what the concept of the place is. If the place is aiming to be inclusive, there are a lot of small things that can help do that. For example, in

Südblock, they always have disclaimers on which they mention that they won't tolerate racism, sexism and homophobia. This is a big thing, because it makes me feel that no matter my skin colour, my religion, my sexuality, I can come here, and no one will judge me.

Another thing that matters is definitely the staff working in those places. People create places. It is not about a building or a street or a neighbourhood, it is about the people who make it. They create the atmosphere, and they build it in a way that will make me feel comfortable or not. I think it is a lot about the people, their attitude, and their approach.

P   Do you think the staff at Südblock shapes the space to their own identity?

D   Yes, the staff here are mainly queer as far as I know. Of course, I think if a space is created for the community by the community, it is a special thing. The staff understand, they are going through the same things that you are going through, and they know how important it is to create a safe space.

P   Is that also something you try to convey with the L-Night meetups?

D   Yes, definitely! The meetups should be inclusive and welcoming. I think that's one of the most important things in our group because we just want everyone to feel welcome and this is how we are trying to do it.

MARTA

M   We are going to Nollendorfplatz, specifically to the subway station there. I have a
very specific memory connected with that
place, which is my first Dyke March. Precisely
the moment when I got out of the subway and
saw all the lesbians coming out of the train,
flooding all the platforms at once.

P   Why did you choose this moment and
place?

M   It represents the first time I realized
how not alone I was. Obviously, I had lesbian
friends before and I went to events, but to have
so much visibility, to participate in an event
specifically directed at me and at people like
me, that was definitely a first.
Moreover, the event took place right after I
moved to Berlin. It was such a great start to
living here. Especially in 2016... There is still a
lot of homophobia and all kinds of phobias in
Poland, but back then it was intensified. To
come to a place where I was so accepted was
groundbreaking and it made me really happy.

P   What did the march represent for you?

M   Firstly, resistance to homophobia,
either direct or in the form of smaller discrim-
inatory practices. The first Dyke March I took
part in happened before marriage equality
was granted. Marriage does not interest me as
such - I don't really want to get married - but
just the fact that I have the possibility like
everybody else to decide is important to me.
The visibility action of the march definitely has
importance too, because that's how you and
others can see that people like you exist and
that it's not just a few voices that demand
change but that there is a powerful movement

standing behind you.

The solidarity that you can feel in the crowd and also all the kinds of emotions that you can feel there struck me. From rage to just being happy and cheerful and grateful. The march encompasses a lot of things for me.

And also obviously the fun part of it, you know - I took the conversation very high-brow - but just the fact that you come out and hang out with your friends and with strangers and you have a very nice and kind of productive evening.

P   What does it mean for you to be present in public space, as a queer person, in the context of a demonstration?

M   It is definitely about reclaiming, because we so often don't feel welcome in public space. Marching in the streets in large numbers is definitely a sign meaning "We're here, this is also our space, we belong here." If there's a few hundreds of you, then your voices are being heard more than if there's just you and your closest friends. It is a sign of resistance, of reclaiming the space, of visibility, of solidarity. A very wholesome political statement.

P   The idea of being stronger when you are with more people is very present in a march and I'm interested in reflecting on how we can make that happen in our smaller projects, in our everyday lives.

M   Definitely. The Dyke March itself can be seen as a little bit exclusionary because it is dedicated to lesbian identifying individuals and queer identifying female individuals.

Bigger solidarity is definitely something we should work on more in the queer community but on the other hand, the message can get dissolved in bigger demonstrations. You have different types of groups and people, all of whom kind of want the same thing but not really. Maybe not in the context of a march itself, because it is important that your own voice and your own needs are heard, but we could definitely figure out other ways to support each other in bigger queer places.

P   Like extra spaces, extra actions?

M   Yes! Or maybe just showing up to the places that you feel you don't belong to. Who knows? You might change your mind. I've been coming to this area a lot now and I do feel kind of welcome. Of course, it would be better if there were more lesbians but then again, if we don't start showing up here, there won't be more of us.

P   Indeed! I really like your take on being in public space as an activist reclaiming action. I can really relate to that. That's why I wanted to do the interviews in public, too. I believe that depending on where you are, just being outside in public space as a queer woman is already political.

M   Definitely. And also discussing your personal queer related stories in public is already a political statement. Obviously, we are being heard by a lot of people passing by here, and I can very well imagine that it can be hard or even dangerous to do this in some cities and places. So, we are lucky, even though we lesbians are not represented that much in this neighborhood, it is nice that we can still have this discussion here.

walking
marching

street
space

personality
characteris

protest
voice

village
not a safe

nation
old-fashio   ept

queer
just a pers

a dead end
a challenge

outside
being with

public spac
a space you   to work
to make you

together
like a very   feeling

legs
getting fr

to notice
to appreci

lesbian
a great pe

EVELYN

E   This area is related to my coming out as a trans woman. When I moved to Berlin, I was living in a work secondment on Kurfürstendamm and at the same time I was experimenting with my gender expression. This is when I decided to come out as a trans woman and go through physical transition. The area around Uhlandstrasse is basically the first time I presented in public as female.

It's also related to a reflection on where I was back then and where I am now. When I left that flat presenting female for the first time, I was utterly terrified. People imagine this as an empowering, exciting moment but actually it was just a moment of sheer terror. And I was wearing these ridiculous high heels! I guess I hadn't really found my style yet and on these cobble streets I was thinking: "Oh my God, if someone tries to attack me right now... I can't run."

I contrast it with where I am now. I'm much more comfortable in my skin, where walking in this area feels normal and natural. It makes me reflect on how far I've come in my transition.

P   How do you feel walking back here?

E   I guess there is a slight nostalgia element to it, but the memory feels quite distant, not too visceral. It brings up a kind of mild feeling. I think the memory feels quite distant from that time now because so much has happened in between.

P   Could you describe how you felt at this moment in this given space?

E   For reference, the route I took was basically: out the door of the building, down one block, cross the road, cross back one block and then down back. It probably took five minutes, but it felt like an eternity.

I did it at night, I think that was part of myself dipping my toe in the water. I didn't want to do it in broad daylight. I guess I still felt kind of ashamed or that I had something to hide. The darkness added to the place feeling like a more threatening space.

Usually walking around these streets, you feel 100% safe because it's a well-to-do area that probably has very little crime. It was just that in that specific moment, it transformed into a much more threatening area for me.

I still had quite a lot of emotional baggage associated with being trans at the time and that also made it feel like a threatening space even though under normal circumstances it wouldn't be.

P   It is like a lens that you put on, and then your whole perspective of the space changes.

E   Exactly.

P   Did something happen?

E   No, no, nothing did happen, it was all fine. I think with presenting authentically as a trans woman, the first time you do it you think "Oh my God, this is crazy, this is scary" - you know, it's not your own thing yet - but every time you do it, it becomes less and less scary until someday it's like you're not even going out "presenting" as female anymore, you're just wearing your clothes and being who you are and that's that.

When I presented as a guy, I did have a certain amount of male privilege insofar as the chances of getting assaulted at night as a man are quite lower than as a woman. I think that maybe - having not grown-up female - I sometimes still carry that kind of male bravado, of just saying "Oh fuck it, who cares? I'll just walk outside at night and nothing's going to happen to me." And I've just been lucky that I've not experienced any kind of incident. My life as a woman has altered that though and I'm sometimes mindful when I'm out on my own late at night, probably being a lot more cavalier in my attitude than I should be.

Also, interestingly enough, I would need to double check this, but I think I used to live there! Which is now an empty space. So, the building I lived in is being demolished, which is news to me! There you go, this area that associates with this specific memory is rapidly changing and I guess the memory will move on with it. It's a nice sort of metaphor.

P   How do you feel seeing this place like that?

E   That time holds a lot of emotional resonance for me, but it's not rooted in that specific flat or building. When I think back about that time, I don't associate it with the area itself but with myself and my personal growth. It's linked to the physical changes that have happened to me rather than the physical changes that have happened to the area.

fence
barrier

territory
hostile

outside
freedom

journey
arduous

crossroads
decisions

closeness
comfort

individuality
expressiveness

marching
protest

queer
radical expression

informa
overwhe

geography
landscape

wandering
thoughtful

direction
aim

itinerant
confused

intimacy
closure

community
LGBTQ+

queer
me

crossroad
direction

locality
community

legs
running

road
freedom

openness
honesty

communication
rency

wait
arrie

spontaneous

ALIX

A   We are going to Platz der Luftbrücke. It's a square near a subway station, with a little parc.
I chose this place because it is the place where the start of my first Dyke March happened. The place is very important for me because it's where I first joined a protest for LGBTQ+ rights that was focussed on and reclaimed by dykes, lesbians, and female-identifying queer people.

C   What was your first impression of the space?

A   That it was so nice to see so many dykes in one place! You would look anywhere and know that you all belonged and that all of you were going to go marching for the same cause and it just felt so good. I met a lot of people there. It also reinforced the bonds I had with the friends I had recently met. It marked a very powerful start of my "queer activities". I'm so fond of this memory because for me, it is very symbolic of the start of my becoming more political and activist about being queer. I kind of see it as a landmark in my life.

C   How is occupying the streets a political action?

A   I think that the march in itself is all about being on the streets and being visible on the streets. I think it's a very efficient way of making yourself visible if you're with a mass of people. We can't be ignored, and we have to be taken into account. I do believe that public space is meant to belong to everyone and yet for a lot of minorities it is not the case, you know. Even saying belonging or not is too extreme, too black and white. The problem is that there is a scale with belonging. It is not like you completely belong or completely don't belong. Sometimes you just don't feel accepted, or it can be harder, you can be humiliated, you can feel unsafe, but it can also be lighter, you just feel uncomfortable. For me, it's about showing these feelings about public space while being in public space. It is the place where you can both be visible and make a statement about being acknowledged.

C   Did you talk with other people than those in your group?

A   Yes! It was so easy to start discussions. I remember I talked with quite a few people. At one point I was in a group of trans women, which was really nice because we just talked about other topics. For example, about the movement called Trans Lives Matter of which I didn't know much about before that. It was really nice to learn. For me, the march was also a place to be educated about different ways of being a lesbian that I didn't know so much about previously.

C   How you can politically occupy public space?

A   Generally, for those of us who are openly out, it is just about being somewhere. And this is enough, actually. It is already a statement; it is already doing something. Concerning the march, I think it is about choosing your location carefully. I read about the Montreal march recently. For their first Dyke March, they chose a very interesting route. They went both to places that were very relevant for them as the lesbian community, lesbian bars, the lesbian or gay neighbourhood... and to places where they felt oppressed, in front of the city hall for example because of gay marriage, or in some parts of the gay neighbourhood which were completely taken over by men. I think in the case of a march it is about having a good mixture of where you go to reinforce the sense of community but also being present in parts of the city where you usually wouldn't be.

C   What was specific to the march in Berlin?

A   I think a certain openness towards breaking the codes of conduct. I felt there was no judgement for what kind of lesbian I was. There was such a huge variety of different people who understood themselves as lesbians.

C   Why was this one protest more important to you, in comparison with others?

A   Because of the lesbians! Because I felt I was protesting for something very personal to me. I mean, it is part of my identity. So, I felt I didn't protest for someone else but for myself for the first time. It felt great, very empowering. I felt the presence of the rest of the community very strongly. I felt very safe, very joyful. I also felt very proud to see all these people who seemed so nice and so friendly and so interesting with their great slogans on their posters. I thought "Wow, I'm part of a good community, we are actually trying to make things a bit better for everyone."
I also really loved the presence of humour and puns in the march. I think there is so much creativity and smartness, wittiness in how a protest can be made. It blew my mind to see how many ways there are to reclaim things, and the place that the queer community gives to humour in this process. I'm still mesmerized by it because I think it is so powerful.

Stair Worship: Heatherwick's Vessel

KEVIN GOTKIN

The January 2018 report released by the New York City Mayoral Advisory Commission on City Art, Monuments, and Markers opens by resisting the idea that controversy around public art is anything new. If anything, a large part of the public outcry about monuments in late 2017 was that there wasn't enough outcry before—that monuments constitute a certain intransigence-in-form and protect public commitments to inequity. "When enough time passes," the Commission co-chairs wrote, "these cast bronze figures start to seem like a natural part of the scenery, the green patina blending with trees and moss.".[1]

Despite the quiet persistence with which monuments become part of the environment—and despite the spate of commissions, reports, and recommendations monumental controversies continue to engender—the discourse is often squarely representationalist. When Henri Lefebvre attempted to name the way hegemony makes use of the social production of space, he was proposing that imaginations of harmony and order are inscribed in "monumental space.".[2] And yet he called this space a "collective mirror" of society ("more faithful than any personal one"), as if monuments naturally and perfectly react to public feeling. It seems that monumental mundanity produces something of a funhouse mirror instead. Beyond monuments, Lefebvre went on to take more interest in what he called the "spatial architectonics" involved in the space-making of quotidian activity—"buildings are to monuments," he wrote, "as everyday life is to festival"—because he assumed monuments are defined by what they represent.[3] But is it actually so easy to separate the texts in public space from a larger texture of public space?

The New York City Commission report recommends several options for addressing the statue of Theodore Roosevelt at the American Museum of Natural History. It notes that Roosevelt was an avowed eugenicist and that the Museum hosted the second and third International Eugenics Congress conferences in 1921 and 1932. Describing Roosevelt, on horseback, towering over two men who walk at his stirrups, it notes that "height is power in public art."

But the report says nothing about the fact that the monument is on a set of stairs.

It says nothing about the other monument to the other President Roosevelt, also made inaccessible by a set of stairs. There is a telling absence of public concern about the fact

Kevin Gotkin, "Stair Worship: Heatherwick's Vessel," in the Avery Review 33 (September 2018), http://averyreview.com/issues/33/stair-worship.

that the Four Freedoms Park that points like an arrow to FDR's bronze bust in New York City—the only memorial to the wheelchair-using president in his home state—is inaccessible to wheelchair users and others who used the same kinds of mobility aids he did at various points during his presidency.[4]

THE SCALING OF JUSTICE

The passage of the Americans with Disabilities Act was spurred in part by a similarly mundane and monumental set of stairs. On March 12, 1990, hundreds of activists gathered in front of the White House to express their outrage about the slow progress of the first landmark omnibus disability rights legislation. It had passed in the Senate but was stuck in the House. The protesters marched to the Capitol, congregating at the base of eighty-two stairs leading up to the building. After speeches and chants, about three dozen activists, part of the organization called ADAPT, got out of their wheelchairs, put down their canes, and made their move toward the stairs.[5]

They climbed. And it wasn't easy. Some nights before, as the action was being planned, several ADAPT members worried it would be demeaning to let nondisabled people see them struggle up the stairs. To others, this was exactly the point[6] The inaccessibility of a built environment designed only for people who take the stairs is exhausting. Reporters and photographers flanked the activists, covered in sweat and heaving.

Tom Olin's [1990] photo of activists climbing the Capitol steps has become iconic in disability protest history. Copyright Tom Olin.

The bill was signed into law months later.

These activists designed their protest using what is called the "social model of disability." This model insists that disability is not an individual, medicalized situation but an active, collective process of sorting some bodies for exclusion. It dislodges disability from particular bodies and locates it within the built environment. And the social model's ur-example is a set of stairs. It is not the use of a wheelchair that disables a person, the model proposes, but the steps at the front of a building.

The social model was a profound refutation of earlier conceptual statuses that had been given to disability. Historical anthropologist Henri-Jacques Stiker has argued that disability in Western twentieth-century history was dominated by newly available notions of replacement, substitution, and compensation. World War I activated rehabilitative contracts between the state and its disabled citizens in ways that in previous periods were mediated through models of divinity or charity. The social model upended them all: Disability isn't actually about bodies at all—it's about the societies that surround and course through them, which are themselves given shape fundamentally by the built environment. The social model identifies the monumentality of stairs as a collective climb that posits a certain upward transcendence. Stairs constitute the muscle memory of prototypical able-bodiedness.

It's important to note, however, that this stair protest did not lead directly to justice. The Capitol Crawl of 1990 is perhaps the most notable event in disability rights, but its focus on legal and legislative change differs significantly from disability justice, a paradigm developed by queer and gender-nonconforming disabled people of color that imagines more radical and transformative framework.[7] The Capitol Crawl activists used the stairs in part to call for the right to independence. Doing so, as disability scholar Hentyle Yapp has written, "appealed to an antiwelfare sentiment targeted against race, particularly blackness.".[8] The ADA stoked a conservative anti-statist desire by seeking the right to work, thus cooperating with ways that welfare support is inequitably gendered and racialized.

Disability scholar Aimi Hamraie has also pointed to the limits of what seem like successes of the rights discourse: In architecture, universal design has been exalted to the point that it no longer acknowledges how central disability was to its formation.[9] The idea that spaces could be designed for all bodies has also made universal design a field that often prizes its depoliticized nature. How to refuse stairs is no simple process.

SOCIAL CLIMBING

In the fall of 2016, a visual effects studio called The Mill was hired by the developer of New York City's Hudson Yards to create a teaser film introducing Thomas Heatherwick's Vessel to the public. The structure is the centerpiece of the Hudson Yards Public Square and Garden on the far west side of Manhattan. The film featured choreography by Matthew Rushing and the Alvin Ailey American Dance Theater—a piece called Rising.

The film is inspired by the "rhythm of a New York morning commute.".[10] It opens with quick shots of a woman on a run, people moving up and down the stairs to an elevated subway line, and then many feet scaling various stairs. Three neighbors leave their brownstones at the same time. They glance at one another at the starting line and then hit their stride. Dancers arrive at the Hudson Yards subway station and work up the stage of the escalator. Outside, they gather at the base of yet another set of stairs where their bodies and outstretched arms form the shadow of the latticework of Vessel. The film ends as this silhouette of the structure fades into the rendering of the project.

Stills from The Mill's teaser film for
Heatherwick Studio's Vessel, 2016.

Vessel is all stairs. Two thousand five hundred individual steps are built into 154 flights of stairs connected by eighty landings. They aren't exactly stairways to nowhere—as an "exclamation point" on the north end of the High Line, Heatherwick imagines that the climb to various landings will offer visitors views of the Hudson and of one another.[11] The diameter of 50 feet at the base expands over the structure's sixteen stories up to a height of 150 feet at its mouth.

The teaser film suggests that Vessel is made not only for, but out of, the public body. As the centerpiece of the public square and gardens, it will be the only non-revenue-producing structure in a giant matrix of commercial and residential tenants. Vessel thus makes literal the private-public partnerships that comprise the body of the Hudson Yards Redevelopment Corporation. Stephen Ross's Related Companies secured its land use from the Metropolitan Transportation Authority, who owns the air rights to the Yards, only after the city borrowed about $3 billion to extend the No. 7 line to the far west side,[12] the city paid $267 million for capital improvements to the business district, and New York state added $25 million in incentives for BlackRock, the largest money manager in the world and one of the development's commercial tenants.[13]

Heatherwick Studio, Vessel, 2016. Rendering by Forbes Massie.

Related also raised about $600 million in construction funding from the EB-5, or Immigrant Investor Program, that confirms eligibility of a green card for foreign investors who can prove their investment in a commercial enterprise and maintain at least ten permanent jobs for US citizens. In order for the Hudson Yards development to qualify in the program, the map used to designate the "targeted employment area" wended upward through Harlem to include several large public housing complexes that qualify the region as a high-unemployment zone.[14] As Nicole Lambrou has noted about Hudson Yards, strategies like these demonstrate the extent to which economic flows determine the capitalist ideology undergirding the image of the contemporary city. The byzantine boundary between public and private development is increasingly legible as the work of capitalism's ideological wand. "The public space is one that you go to," Lambrou writes, "to plug into the larger flow of investment, capital, and an image of urban lifestyle.".[15]

Stephen Ross handpicked Vessel as part of the public's return on its investment, the part of the return that doesn't include actual repayment to the city or state. And Heatherwick offers the city a literal manifestation of urban renewal as a rehabilitative process—a structure to make people sweat.

The project's aesthetic of collective fitness is clearly tied to Heatherwick's lifelong fascination with the climbing frame, or what Americans call the jungle gym. "New Yorkers have a fitness thing," he's said.[16] And whether people perceive the jungle gym, Indian stepwells, or a honeycomb (the most common responses to what Ted Loos in the New York Times called "the city's biggest Rorschach test"), there is a curiously uninterrogated association between the design and the salubrious quality of working and being out of breath.[17] In its promotion, Ross has called it by its nickname: the social climber.[18]

BREATHLESS PATRIOTISM

Vessel is celebrated by declarations that it is "interactive," though a more accurate understanding would have it as "anti-active": limiting, by design, anyone whose body doesn't easily climb stairs. Vessel is only interactive if you imagine one charmed visitor-figure: the young, bipedal, non-suicidal, stroller-less, luggage-less climber who cultivates a group of similarly embodied climbers for the trek. How does this categorical subject ascend so effortlessly?

The Hudson Yards development and American ideologies of ability grew together in the later twentieth century. "Ablenationalism" is what disability scholars name as the way that able-bodiedness is made to seem natural, unmarked, and intrinsic to the imagination of US citizenship and culture—and how a narrow set of disabled people have been selected for entry into global consumer culture in the name of inclusion.[19] Disability imagined as a corroborating converse to notions of moral fitness allows inclusion to be measured through the limited notion of exception, thus maintaining existing injustices.

Disability developed within an emerging neoliberal order as Hudson Yards, too, reflected neoliberal imperatives. Proposals like a 1964 deal to build a sprawling middle-income complex for twelve thousand families were stalled and repeatedly tabled in the face of the complexity of managing the necessary private-public financing partnerships.[20] Rankling administration after administration, Hudson Yards started to feel like a challenging climb.

In the 1970s, marathons boomed in the United States. The number of entrants in the New York City Marathon surged roughly 10,000 percent between 1970 and 1981.[21] It's also in the 1970s when hundreds of "thru-hikers" began attempting the full length of the Appalachian Trail in a single effort, part of what sport historian Adam Berg calls the "new strenuosity" in American culture.[22]

And then there was the mosaic of community events that took up the marathon's suffix during the dawn of the American nonprofit-industrial complex that found rituals of collective vigorous physical activity to be supremely useful charity fundraising tools: the Jerry Lewis Muscular Dystrophy Association Telethon saw viewership ratings higher than the Super Bowl[23] and more than five combined nights of television's most highly rated show of the time, Roots.[24] The March of Dimes' annual walkathons saw hundreds of thousands of participants in major cities, using incipient pledge and sponsorship fundraising models to cathect young marching bodies with the capacity to extract civic capital from their communities.

Sydney Pollack's 1969 dance marathon drama, They Shoot Horses, Don't They?, starred Jane Fonda as the depressive figure of endurance, ultimately murdered in supposed compassion by her partner. The film adaptation of Horace McCoy's 1935 novel played as a suggestive, post-Vietnam existentialist echo of the 1930s Depression. On the other side of the decade, Fonda had pioneered an at-home VHS tape fitness boom with Jane Fonda's Workout Book in 1981 and Jane Fonda's Workout in VHS in 1982.

These developments in the 1970s were contemporaneous with the neoliberalism that determines America's political, economic, and affective modes. The -thon-ification of the United States since the 1970s demonstrates the ways that American patriotism as a civic religion is undergirded by fantasies of physical autonomy and independence. The stairs are a site of American worship. Vessel tells this story of American able-nationalism in both content and form, and when it came time for the construction ritual of "topping out" of the structure in December 2017, the American flag affixed to the final piece of steel took on particular resonance. The project summited its own semantic and material ascendance.

WHAT TO DO WITH MISSTEPS

The topping out of Vessel. Courtesy of Related Companies and Oxford Properties.

Ironically, at the time of Vessel's opening, New York City is also home to a burgeoning scene of disability arts, with artists that take up the category of non-normative physical and mental embodiments to produce game-changing artistic innovations. At a recent sold-out three-night run at New York Live Arts, the disability-centric dance company Kinetic Light used a large ramp to produce novel choreographic forms in wheeled movement. Park McArthur's Passive Vibration Durometer Facts, recently on view at Essex Street on the Lower East Side, featured laminated rubber loading dock bumpers installed at a height of 48 inches above street level. Because the gallery's main entrance opens onto a set of stairs that descends to the exhibition space, the height of the pieces calls attention to the ways that taking the stairs is often taken for granted for bipedal guests. McArthur's investigation about the knowledge we can find in the materiality of accessibility—and an intricate erotics of the beatings it takes—includes depth and height as easily ignored categories.

107

Meanwhile, Heatherwick seems to treat the accessibility of Vessel with the woefully limited ruler of the ADA. There will be a glass elevator to transport visitors to the top, checking the box of the regulations but not honoring the spirit of the law. Bloomberg and several other news outlets reported in the fall of 2016 that only physically disabled visitors will be permitted to use it.[25] Though disability determinations besiege federal and state bureaucracies, Heatherwick imagines these will be made at the entrance to the elevator, leaving visitors with strollers, luggage, and nonapparent disabilities without much certainty about their access to the structure.[26]

It's tempting to cast Vessel close to its etymological roots: that which is, in the end, empty. It's easy to refuse the claim that the vessel moves things, moving New Yorkers without moving itself. But in fact Vessel is quite full—with the imaginations that constitute ableism and with fantasies about who can and will inhabit public space. And it's even easier to imagine that the structure will move New Yorkers to protest, filled with an array of vibrant cultural actors who take disability seriously.

[1]
Mayoral Advisory Commission on City Art, Monuments, and Markers, "Report to the City of New York," January 2018, https://www1.nyc.gov/assets/monuments/downloads/pdf/mac-monuments-report.pdf.

[2]
Henri Lefebvre, *The Production of Space* [1974], trans. Donald Nicholson-Smith (Cambridge, MA: Basil Blackwell, 1991), 220–222.

[3]
Lefebvre, *The Production of Space*, 223.

[4]
Perhaps the most memorable element about the monumentalizing of FDR is the relegated representation of his disability at his presidential memorial in Washington, D.C. A large cloak covers his chair in one statue, and another, more clearly showing wheels, was added four years after the memorial opened.

[5]
Leonard Davis, *Enabling Acts: The Hidden Story of How the Americans with Disabilities Act Gave the Largest US Minority Its Rights* (Boston, MA: Beacon Press, 2015), 214.

[6]
Michael Winters, "I Was There, Washington, D.C., 1990," ADAPT, link.

[7]
For more on this distinction, see Sins Invalid, Skin, Tooth, and Bone—The Basis of Our Movement is People: A Disability Justice Primer, 2016, https://www.flipcause.com/secure/reward/OTMxNQ==.

[8]
Hentyle Yapp, "Disability as Exception: China, Race, and Human Rights," *American Quarterly.* vol. 69, no. 3 (September 2017): 637.

[9]
Aimi Hamraie, *Bulding Access: Universal Design and the Politics of Disability* (Minneapolis: University of Minnesota Press, 2017).

[10]
"Behind the Project: Hudson Yards 'Vessel' Film," *The Mill*, September 16, 2016, http://www.themill.com/millchannel/876/behind-the-project%3A-hudson-yards-%27vessel%27-film-.

[11]
"Vessel, The Centerpiece of the Hudson Yards Public Square and Gardens, Tops Out Reaching Full Height," Hudson Yards New York, December 6, 2017, https://www.hudsonyardsnewyork.com/press-releases/vessel-the-centerpiece-of-the-hudson-yards-public-square-and-gardens-tops-out-reaching-full-height/.

[12]
Jim Dwyer, "Hudson Yards Offered a Payday for the Subway, but We Got Offices," the *New York Times*, June 15, 2017, https://www.nytimes.com/2017/06/15/nyregion/hudson-yards-property-taxes-subway-offices.html.

[13]
Greg David, "The Story of Hudson Yards Is Now the Story of New York," *Crain's New York*, June 4, 2018, https://www.crainsnewyork.com/article/20180604/BLOGS01/180609992/the-story-of-hudson-yards-is-now-the-story-of-new-york.

[14]
Kriston Capps, "Inside EB-5, the Cash-for-Visas Program Luxury Developers Love," *CityLab*, May 9, 2017, https://www.citylab.com/equity/2017/05/kushner-companies-real-estate-and-eb-5-cash-for-visas-reform/525792/.

[15]
Nichole Lambrou, "Hudson Yards: A Sustainable Micropolis," the *Avery Review* 22 (March 2017), http://averyreview.com/issues/22/hudson-yards-a-sustainable-micropolis.

[16]
Ted Loos, "A $150 Million Stairway to Nowhere on the Far West Side," the *New York Times*, September 14, 2016, https://www.nytimes.com/2016/09/15/arts/design/hudson-yards-own-social-climbing-stairway.html.

[17]
Loos, "A $150 Million Stairway to Nowhere."

[18]
Shawn Tully, "This Monument Could Be Manhattan's Answer to the Eiffel Tower," *Fortune*, September 14, 2016, http://fortune.com/2016/09/14/stephen-ross-eiffel-tower-hudson-yards/.

[19]
David Mitchell and Sharon Snyder, *The Biopolitics of Disability: Neoliberalism, Ablenationalism, and Peripheral Embodiment* (Ann Arbor: University of Michigan Press, 2015).

[20]
Robert E. Bedingfield, "US Steel Weighs Midtown Project," *the New York Times*, August 1, 1964, 1, 34.

[21]
Pamela Cooper, *The American Marathon* (Syracuse: Syracuse University Press, 1998), 141.

[22]
Adam Berg, "'To Conquer Myself': The New Strenuosity and the Emergence of 'Thru-hiking' on the Appalachian Trail in the 1970s," *Journal of Sport History*, vol. 42, no. 1 (Spring 2015): 1–19.

[23]
"Jerry Lewis Labor Day Telethon—The First Eleven Years," 1977 (New York: Muscular Dystrophy Association, Inc.), quoted in Lawrence Joseph Londino, "A Descriptive Analysis of 'The Jerry Lewis Labor Day Telethon for Muscular Dystrophy" (doctoral dissertation, University of Michigan, 1978), 63.

[24]
Telethon Topics, October 14, 1977 (New York: Muscular Dystrophy Association, Inc.), 2, quoted in Londino, "A Descriptive Analysis of 'The Jerry Lewis Labor Day Telethon for Muscular Dystrophy," 6.

[25]
Katya Kazakina and David M. Levitt, "Related Unveils Design for Towering $150 Million 'Vessel' in Hudson Yards," *Bloomberg*, September 14, 2016, https://www.bloomberg.com/news/articles/2016-09-14/related-unveils-design-for-towering-heatherwick-vessel-in-hudson-yards.

[26]
(And then there's another relationship to disability that Heatherwick seems not to have addressed: how the low railings will safely hold its climbers.)

Stair Worship Addendum:

A conversation between Shannon Finnegan & Kevin Gotkin

SHANNON FINNEGAN &
KEVIN GOTKIN

In March of 2021, two years after Shannon Finnegan organised *Anti-Stairs Club Lounge* at *the Vessel*, and three years after Kevin Gotkin published *Stair Worship* in *Avery Review*, Shannon and Kevin joined in conversation to reflect upon the position of their work and writing today, and to discuss the shorter and longer-term impacts of the Vessel. The conversation can be read both as an addendum to Kevin's original *Stair Worship* essay, as well as a standalone dialogue on the place the Vessel continues to hold socially and politically now over two years after its public opening.

S   One thing that I am curious about—partially for my own knowledge—is how you first heard about the Vessel?

K   I wasn't following the developments of the Vessel from the early stages. It was only when I started writing about it that I discovered the long history of the attempts to redevelop Hudson Yards. It's remarkable that there were decades of failed development proposals preceding the Vessel. I was approached by Jacob Moore, a Contributing Editor at The Avery Review, and he explained that they wanted to feature writing about disability for their architecture readership and proposed the Vessel as a piece to review. I am not an architecture scholar, so I didn't know who Thomas Heatherwick was. But then I realized the Vessel and the problems that were associated with it, were things that really connected to a lot of my own research and it's a good example of the way that ableism happens when it's not labelled ableism.

I'm mostly focused on the places where values about bodies and minds are created in a supposedly neutral or apolitical space. One of the things that I think about a lot is how the legacy of the disability rights movement has produced disability as this minority category—as something very important and powerful, but a supposedly smaller subsection of the world. And that just has never made sense to me, this minoritisation of disability, because I think its frameworks enrol everybody in knowledges about disability. For my review, I wasn't trying to write a call-out or a take-down but a piece that would ask *"Hey, isn't it curious that ableism happens in these ways that go completely unnoticed and unnamed?"*, and, in doing so, how does the silence around an all-stairs proposal get so far?

A lot of that is down to—and I write about this in the piece—the political economy of the project. Processes of rezoning and redistricting were enacted to qualify the project for different kinds of public funding. There was even the trading of green cards for funds. It's wild! And of course, it's in the private sector, so there's no real public antagonism, no meaningful community engagement or feedback. Once I started writing about it, I saw things happen in real-time, like colleagues being invited into rooms with city agencies trying to do some damage control. To me, those developments were just further proof of how far we go in not antagonizing a troubling premise for an architectural concept. And when you think critically about a project like this, you realize the built, material environment conceals and black boxes its ideological functions. What makes it supposedly beautiful? Where did it come from? Who was paid? Who got the contracts?

S   Yes, exactly.

K   How did you come to stage the Anti-Stairs Club Lounge[1] at the Vessel?

S   I don't remember how I first heard about the Vessel. It might have been through your piece because it was published while it was still under construction. I remember I started to hear murmurings about it. I had done another version of Anti-Stairs

Club Lounge at the Wassaic Project, so I already had this concept of the Anti-Stairs Club Lounge in my mind.

I felt really angry about the Vessel. We're often told that things can't be accessible because it's too expensive or because of existing structures. And so to see something so expensive built in this area that hadn't been developed, I just felt enraged by that. And I was like, *"oh, these two things fit together— Anti-Stairs Club Lounge and a monument of stairs."*

From there, it was a process of reimagining Anti-Stairs Club Lounge to fit that space. I knew that I wanted to do it very soon after the Vessel opened, so I started to monitor it. I signed up for Hudson Yards' publicity emails. I did a deep dive into the materials on their website. I had my partner reach out to get an official response about the elevator policy. I visited while it was still under construction, and things like that. I was trying to figure out what the rules of the space would be, because parts of that area are a public park and parts are a privately owned public space (POPS), so I wasn't sure exactly where the Lounge would happen. I wanted to create the sense of a lounge, while evading the rules and policies of the space whilst also making something that would be very easy to dismantle and pack up if we were asked to leave.

Externally facing protests where you're showing up some-where to educate people about that space, was never for me. I was more interested in enacting an alternative—showing what I hope for from public space. Which is that I want to have places to rest, I want to be able to lounge, and I want to be able to be to-gether with others. All things which the Vessel does not offer.

Anti-Stairs Club Lounge happened a week after the opening of the Vessel, so initial reviews and publicity were happening and then continuing to happen afterwards. I noticed it was very widely criticized, there was a lot of negative writing and attention on the Vessel, but a lot of that did not acknowledge access as part of the critique. Instead, it said things like *"it's ugly"*, *"it's a playground for the rich"*, *"it's just about Instagram"*. All things that, yes, seemed very true, but kind of like you were saying Kevin, ableism wasn't being named as part of the way that space was created.

K   I think it's important to locate the Anti-Stairs Club Lounge within several artistic legacies. One is the tradition of mobile installation. Mobile libraries or pop-up exhibitions make impermanence crucial in expanding notions of the gallery and the exhibition space. Bringing out into the world something that is not going to live there forever.

But then it also connects to the legacy of institutional critique. And it reminds me a lot of Park McArthur's work, *Projects 195* at MoMA where so much of the artistry is in the imaginative space created by the disabled artist considering how the resources from the institution could have been used otherwise. I think it is very much what we all experienced in being there for the Anti-Stairs Club Lounge. It's setting down the conditions for a totally different use of this space.

The third tradition, of course, is protest artistry. And that helps me think through some of the most fascinating parts of being a participant of the Anti-Stairs Club Lounge at the Vessel. You had a real confounding of the security apparatus at the Vessel. I think they would have been happier in a way to see us angrier because that would have aligned with a certain framework and maybe there's a protocol for that they could have responded with if we had behaved in a certain way. But we weren't identifiably protesting. In fact, there were some seasoned disability rights activists who thought we should be chanting. That was interesting to watch among the group. To consider how we channel, as you're saying, the rage and the affect. I think it was so difficult because it wasn't really resistance. It was designating an imaginative space for connections to emerge, like people talking and hanging out and being comfortable. Like bringing cushions, as you did. This was something that protest itself doesn't usually make happen. Protest artistry is so much about the able-bodied—the hyper-able-bodied endurance subject coming out and marching, getting into the streets. And here we have a departure from that.

I think what's amazing is how that piece sits within those three legacies, which means that it's always legible, to some extent, without giving you this perfect characteristic. I think what was so exciting for every-body was that it felt like you were in the middle of the be-coming of something, maybe one of the only public moments of antagonism around this thing.

S   Yeah, a few things came up for me when thinking back to the Anti-Stairs Club Lounge at the Vessel. First of all, I'm so happy that you brought up Park's piece, because that piece was so present for me when I was thinking about the Vessel. Especially the piece *PARA-SITES*, where there's an imagining of a live-work space for disabled artists.[2] It made me think about what could have been built in place of the Vessel, or what could have happened with those resources.

And I also love what you said about the security, because I remember talking to Pelenakeke Brown about an interaction that she had with a security guard. He really wanted to show her the elevator as a way of proving the space was accessible. I feel really excited about the refusal of engagement or attention. Of just being like: *"No, I'm not trying to participate in your ableist system or structure. We're going to do our thing over here, instead."* That has been an important part of the different iterations of Anti-Stairs Club Lounge.

K   And that brings up another part of the installation, which was the agreement or contract of non-engagement. Maybe we could locate some of these things, and some of the elements of Park's show that we've been talking about, within the imagined space of material resistance when there are no materials. Park was thinking through MoMA's expansion into this luxury condominium, which is backed by the same kind of money that Related Properties, the real estate company behind the Vessel, is also involved in. What do we do to bring critical engagement when the sources of the resources are not bringing it themselves? I think it's so cool to have everyone feel like they are signing something that gives you a little bit of the power that is otherwise shrouded in mystery and set off far away from the public. In the signing of the agreement there's a ritualistic moment saying, *"I promise I'm not going to"*, in the company of witnesses to help make this commitment not to go up the Vessel. When we are giving up on trying to engage with institutions as they usually operate, it's the creation of these other, more powerful mechanisms for critique and refusal that might not actually have any kind of binding legal properties, but that make such a huge impact.

I think all of this is also a post-ADA feeling. The Americans with Disabilities Act turned 30 in 2020 and there was a lot of introspection in the disability community about what it has wrought. And one of the things, in almost every institution of American life, is the way the ADA brings a compliance-minded approach and a focus on the law when we think about wrongs in disability service provisions. We always rush to the lawsuit as the imagined area of redress. Though that has been very powerful in securing transformations of public space and public accommodation, it still holds to an idea of how change can work that I think often further propagates ableist thinking. So in the case of the Vessel, the developers had to meet with city officials and there was a strong threat of litigation as an advocacy tool. It is really the ADA, I think, that casts the shadow over everything, and it becomes really difficult to imagine other ways of engaging in a space like this that isn't about a potential lawsuit.

So I think the agreement to not collaborate with the Vessel in any way, shape, or form is another kind of imaginative dimension that questions how we get out of these frameworks of knowledge about disability that are actually quite limited.

S   Well with the Vessel, there eventually was a legal agreement[3] between the Southern Manhattan District Attorney's Office and the Vessel, and my understanding is that it requires the installation of a second lift mechanism to be installed on the top of the Vessel, to give access to more varied vistas, I guess.

I remember when that agreement was announced, it felt like way too little, too late. Adding an additional lift system doesn't even really make sense to me. I think part of what your article does so well is to show that ableism is so deeply rooted in that structure. Adding another lift system doesn't fix that. And it remains to be seen, especially now with the financial trouble that Hudson Yards is facing,[4] whether that will be enforceable and how exactly that will happen.

   One other thing that is interesting to me about the agreement is that Related Properties still do not concede that ADA rules apply to the Vessel. They said, *"we want to make it more accessible. We will agree to do these things, but we're not saying that ADA applies to this."* Part of what I've understood behind this distinction, in the mind of Related Properties, is that the Vessel is an artwork and that's one reason why the ADA would not apply to it. As an artist that is both fascinating and horrifying to me. The idea that art could be used as a defence against increased access is so different from what I have experienced in the disability arts community, which is using art as a wedge to insert or increase access.

K   The ADA generates all of these imaginations of exemption. Another major example is in the provision of a technology service, which is the way that Uber and Lyft have resisted ADA compliance. Instead of having to actually make things ADA accessible, they say it doesn't apply to what they do. They say, *"we actually don't supply cars and transportation. What we do is offer access to an app."* So other laws might apply to the digital accessibility of the app, but in terms of actually requiring that there be wheelchair-accessible vehicles, that's not something that the ADA can legislate, making it another fascinating refusal of what is imagined to be this administrative burden.

At its best, the ADA offers a framework for engagement. The actual ADA guidelines are not so much about particular figures, although there are some that emerge. It's actually more about how bodies use the space in this specific situation for what the space is intended to do. And people still think of the ADA as this checklist when really, it's an interrogative framework, or aspires to be. And actually, it could be a lot easier for places to think more expansively and creatively without any of that imagined burden if they could just actually do engagement and collaboration correctly.

It's always the recourse to some kind of free market that the ADA seems to get in the way of. The Vessel is this dedicated public space next to an enormous new mall. And in a weird way, malls have been, and can be, very accessible because they're huge, and you're supposed to easily get lost in their smooth surfaces. But in this case, it's a kind of counter-ballast. The Vessel becomes this thing that is supposed to counter the blatant market mentality of the entire development. The Vessel stands in for what the public gets out of this intense built environment of the capitalist market structure. What an incredibly twisted logic, that to claim denials of access, is somehow infringing access to capital circulation.

S   I want to talk about what's happened recently, which is that the Vessel is now closed because there have been three suicides there.[5] Which is something that you marked in your article as part of the ableist assumptions of that structure. It's unclear when it will reopen, and I've been noticing in the Hudson Yards emails that where the Vessel used to be an icon in its heading, and it's now been taken out. There seems to be a turn away from the Vessel as the central iconography of the Hudson Yards brand. Another thing that I've also noticed in some of the dialogue that I've witnessed about the closure is a separation of access concerns about the Vessel and the suicides that have happened, instead of seeing those as part of the same thing.

K   My earlier drafts of *Stair Worship* had a much more direct naming of the possibility of suicide, and I edited a lot of it out. The Vessel hadn't opened at that point, and we were looking at the renderings, but it was still very clear to me that the railings would be low. I've survived a suicide attempt, so as a writer, I'm always trying to think of an ethics of care around signalling the reference in itself. Content warnings and trigger warnings are to me really inadequate as a preface. Sometimes it feels like an offloading of the duty. *"I'm about to talk about suicide take care of yourself!"* But what do you actually do to take care of your reader? I think the line was about a deferral or a refusal of the obligation to make sure people are safely held. I think what happened is more of this momentum of silence, where everyone tries to quiet down. I wonder if I should have mentioned it as another example of ableist design that doesn't get named as such.

       I'm pretty sure soon the Vessel will announce a retrofitting plan. And especially with the case of the Vessel, where there's a literal vessel that opens at the top, they're going to have difficulty retrofitting with a safety apparatus that doesn't, for them, somehow compromise the openness of the structure. This distinction between aesthetics and access continues to make problems and literally becomes fatal as a result.

S   I always wonder about Thomas Heatherwick in all of this. The interviews with him are so wild. I listened to one interview where he said he made the Vessel to *"bring people together"*[6]— what?!

It feels to me like such an extreme prioritization of aesthetics. A singular idea that works for the designers and is therefore assumed to be universal. It remains a question to me—how does that space move forward? Certainly the Vessel, but also all of Hudson Yards, the luxury condos and offices and mall.

K   It occurs to me with Heatherwick that the process behind the construction of the Vessel is a really good example of the culture of anti-interdependence in architecture. The whole field is based on people's names. Everyone goes and toils into extreme burnout in order to one day maybe get licensed to go build your own firm with your name on it. And Heatherwick is one of the most famous, one of the biggest names in the independence-mindedness of the profession.

He's called the Vessel, the "social climber." And climbing for him seems to be an architectural metaphor. I wonder to what extent he might be thinking of climbing as something that you have to do in architecture to make it. There's this intense hierarchy and expertise that is designed by authority systems. Heatherwick imagines that the Vessel is supposed to bring people together to climb. Isn't it so New York to be out of breath, rushing from place to place? So it's both New York and this lionization of the exhausted artist. The fundamentally collaborative nature of architecture is obscured by all this hero worship.

S   One other thing that I wanted to flag is that in some ways it's easy to look at the Vessel, which is such an extreme form of inaccessible design, and feel like it is an isolated incident. But we're seeing it happen over and over. There was the Hunters Point Library in Queens,[7] where the fiction section was only accessible via stairs. There was the Olafur Eliasson piece at the Tate,[8] where there were stairs at its entrypoint. There was Jeremy Deller's Peterloo Memorial...[9]

"The stair" is such a specific symbol in disability activism. It's such a legible symbol of inaccessibility. In a lot of disability spaces I'm a part of, there's a sense of, yes, of course we need to think about stairs and ramps, but we also need to be thinking about access much more expansively. And then, outside of disability-centred spaces too, to see what feels like a very clear and obvious mistake, being made repeatedly. It's this strange feeling of very separate spheres of thinking about access.

K   The FDR monument on Roosevelt Island is another example. FDR used a wheelchair, and you can't access the tip of the point where you actually see his bust unless you mount some stairs. The stair is such a figure in the history of disability. But it's bemusing to think about why some of these examples get so much attention when every block in New York City features some kind of inaccessible design, especially in residential design. It seems like we put all of our attention on these things without noting that the distribution of these inequities is so profoundly ubiquitous.

S   Yes, absolutely. One of my favourite parts of the project was that people could keep their hats, these bright orange Anti-Stairs Club Lounge beanies, and wear them in their daily lives. I love wearing mine in the subway because the inaccessibility there is so upsetting and having my own little protest while I'm there feels cathartic. But yes, I think you're right that inaccessibility gets imagined in these symbolic spaces, when in fact it's everywhere around us.

K   The beanies are another example of the way that the Anti-Stairs Club Lounge produced a distribution of a kind of subversive aesthetics. Most people who have hats from that protest/performance piece wear them everywhere! Which is a suggestion that the Anti-Stairs Club Lounge could be here, it could be here, it could be... like subjunctive tense. Like waiting. Should it be here? I think it created a real sense of pride for people who were there. The legibility of the symbol without, that doesn't announce what it is, just the stairs crossed out, is so evocative. When I see people looking at mine, I wonder what they're thinking. What is this activating for them?

For me that's a real space of hope. We're talking a lot about the hulking institutions that are so good at resistance to antagonism that you do have to wonder, where do we find hope? But I think we have these rhizomatic structures and networks for producing subversive aesthetics that are critical, that do interrogate these systems, and that's where I put a lot of my own hope. Which is why I think disability artistry is the way to think through disability politics generally, and politics even more generally than that. It's in the production and distribution and circulation of these aesthetics that we begin. It's one way that we can use impossibility to actually train our political instincts. It's a way for us to think about what is possible, despite the feeling that we're never going to get it all. And even if we don't get it all, it doesn't mean we give up hope, it doesn't mean that we say, *"Screw all that."* It's this automation and distribution of the possible, that sense of a possibility, that I think your work and a lot of the disabled artists working in New York and around the world are producing right now that continues to generate hope.

Shannon Finnegan and Kevin Gotkin, March 2021

[1]

For more information on Anti-Stairs Club Lounge, see: https://shannonfinnegan.com/anti-stairs-club-lounge-at-the-vessel

[2]

Park McArthur. Live-Work Residence. 2018 https://www.moma.org/audio/playlist/55/816

[3]

Article: Manhattan U.S. Attorney Announces Agreement With Related Companies To Increase Accessibility Of The Vessel In Hudson Yards, United States Department of Justice; https://www.justice.gov/usao-sdny/pr/manhattan-us-attorney-announces-agreement-related-companies-increase-accessibility

[4]

Article: Pandemic Economy Could Turn A Deserted Hudson Yards Into An Even Bigger Taxpayer Money Pit, Gothamist; https://gothamist.com/news/pandemic-economy-could-turn-deserted-hudson-yards-even-bigger-taxpayer-money-pit

[5]

Article: 150-Foot Vessel Sculpture at Hudson Yards Closes After 3rd Suicide, NY Times; https://www.nytimes.com/2021/01/12/nyregion/hudson-yards-suicide-vessel.html

[6]

Article: "Thomas Heatherwick designed the Vessel to "bring people together", Dezeen; https://www.dezeen.com/2019/03/22/thomas-heatherwick-studio-vessel-hudson-yards-movies/

[7]

Article: The New $41 Million Hunters Point Library Has One Major Flaw, Gothamist; https://gothamist.com/news/new-41-million-hunters-point-library-has-one-major-flaw

[8]

Article: Wheelchair User Criticizes Tate Modern for Inaccessibility Issues at Olafur Eliasson Exhibition, Hyperallergic; https://hyperallergic.com/513173/wheelchair-user-criticizes-tate-modern-for-at-olafur-eliasson/

[9]

Article: Jeremy Deller Peterloo monument unveiled amid disability row, BBC News; https://www.bbc.com/news/entertainment-arts-49333004

A house in the Dutch East Indies

Een huis in Indië

PAOLETTA HOLST

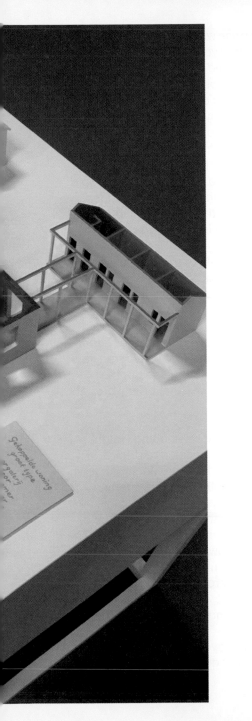

133

They looked at me with surprise when I told them that I had come from Brussels. 'When you travel long distances frequently, you get used to it' I replied. I found that the hours on the road often became a kind of vacuum within the experience of a day, and, as is routine, they would rarely leave behind any specific impression unless something remarkable happened. Whilst in such a vacuum on the train back home from this day, I realised what I'd experienced just two hours previously had indeed been quite remarkable. That day, which I would otherwise certainly have forgotten, had taken a sudden turn because of a curious encounter with a group of people in the museum café at Sophiahof in The Hague.

In the morning, I had taken the train to the administrative city of The Netherlands to apply for a visa at the Indonesian Embassy for an upcoming trip to Java and had decided to visit the recently opened museum Sophiahof afterwards. I had read on their website that Sophiahof *seeks to illuminate the implications of the colonial past in the Dutch East Indies for the Netherlands of today*, and I was curious to see how that would translate into an exhibition. In the end it was the meeting and not the exhibition,—little of which I remember now—that briefly brought the colonial past disturbingly close.

Since I had some time to spare and was hoping I might strike up a conversation with someone, I decided to drink a coffee in the museum café after seeing the exhibition. I sat down at one of the tables, on a bench against the wall. An elderly lady with red lipstick and striking earrings seated at the table next to me spoke in a hushed voice to the waitress behind the bar. Both smiled and nodded warmly in my direction as I sat down. The long wall behind me was covered in blown-up copies of black-and-white photos from the colonial era, interspersed with portraits of everyday life in today's Indonesia. I ordered a coffee and was persuaded to try an "Indies Pastry", which looked sweet but turned out to be savoury. 'Delicious,' I muttered.

'You've come a long way, haven't you?' the waitress asked. 'Your accent?' she inquired, seeing my questioning expression.

Ze hadden me met verbazing aangekeken toen ik vertelde dat ik vanuit Brussel was gekomen. 'Als je vaker lange afstanden reist,' had ik geantwoord 'dan raak je er wel aan gewend.' Dan worden de uren onderweg een soort vacuüm in de beleving van je dag, en laten ze, zoals routine, zelden een specifieke indruk achter, tenzij er iets opmerkelijks gebeurt. Dat laatste had ik niet uitgesproken, maar ik weet nog dat ik me in de trein terug naar huis realiseerde, dat hetgeen wat ik nog geen twee uur geleden had meegemaakt toch best opmerkelijk was geweest. De dag, die ik anders zeer zeker vergeten zou zijn, had namelijk een plotse wending gekregen door een merkwaardige ontmoeting met enkele mensen in het museum café van het Sophiahof in Den Haag.

Ik was die ochtend met de trein naar de regeringsstad gegaan om daar bij de Indonesische ambassade een visum aan te vragen voor een reis naar Java en besloot om daarna een bezoek te brengen aan het recent geopende museum. Op hun website had ik gelezen dat het Sophiahof "de betekenis van het koloniale verleden van Nederlands-Indië voor het Nederland van nu wil belichten" en ik was benieuwd om te zien hoe zich dat in een tentoonstelling zou vertalen. Het bleek uiteindelijk de ontmoeting en niet de tentoonstelling,—waar ik me nu niet zo veel meer van kan herinneren—die het koloniale verleden even verontrustend dichtbij haalde.

Omdat ik nog tijd over had en hoopte met iemand een gesprek te kunnen aanknopen stapte ik na het zien van de tentoonstelling het museum café binnen. Ik zette mij aan een van de tafeltjes op een bank tegen de muur. Naast mij zat een oude dame met rood gestifte lippen en opvallende oorbellen die op gedempte toon kletste met de bediende achter de bar. Ze glimlachten en knikte beiden vriendelijk mijn kant op toen ik mij geïnstalleerd had. De lange muur achter mij was bedrukt met uitvergrote kopieën van zwart-wit foto's uit de koloniale tijd, afgewisseld met portretten van het dagelijks leven in het Indonesië van nu.

Ik bestelde een koffie en werd overgehaald om er een "Indisch gebakje" bij te nemen, dat er zoet uitzag maar hartig bleek te zijn.

'Heerlijk,' mompelde ik.

'Yes, I'm from Brussels.' I told her I had to apply for my visa here because I'm Dutch. After I'd taken a few bites of the pastry and was about to ask them what they thought of the exhibition, three elderly men entered. Chatting loudly, they sat down at the table opposite me. The waitress sighed, walked over to their table and took their order. The men seemed to be entertained by a book that one of them had produced from his pocket and placed on the table.

'I think it's a photo album,' the woman beside me whispered. She had turned towards me when she noticed how curiously I was eyeing the men.

'Oh really?' I whispered back, not knowing what else to say.

'Yes, look.'

I turned to look and, indeed, could see one of the men turning a page of the album and unfolding what looked like a floor plan.

'Our old house in Semarang!' he exclaimed.

'Oh, Semarang,' exclaimed the woman beside me. 'Do you know Semarang?' she asked.

'Only from books,' I replied, 'but I've never been there. I'm going there soon.'

'Oh, that's nice. A beautiful city, Semarang.'

My plan was indeed to travel to Semarang as part of my research into colonial houses and residential culture in the late colonial period. In the second decade of the twentieth century Semarang was the first municipality in the Dutch Indies to draw up large-scale urban expansion plans and public housing projects. In publications from that period written by H.F. Tillema, a passionate chemist, businessman, amateur photographer, and advocate for better hygiene conditions in the colony, I had come across plans and countless photographs of these new development projects, accompanied by statistical data that charted mortality rates as a result of epidemics and infectious

'Je komt zeker van ver?' vroeg de vrouw achter de bar. 'Je accent,' zei ze, toen ze mijn vragende blik zag.

'Ja, ik kom uit Brussel,' en ik vertelde dat ik mijn visum hier moest aanvragen omdat ik Nederlander ben.

Toen ik na een paar happen op het punt stond om hen naar hun mening over de tentoonstelling te vragen, stapte er drie oude mannen binnen. Luidruchtig discussiërend namen ze plaats aan het tafeltje tegenover mij. Met een zucht stapte de bediende achter de bar vandaan en nam hun bestelling op. De mannen leken zich te amuseren over een boek dat een van hen uit zijn tas haalde en op tafel legde.

'Ik geloof dat het een fotoalbum is,' fluisterde de dame me toe. Ze had zich naar mij toe gebogen toen ze zag dat ik de mannen nieuwsgierig bestudeerde.

'O ja?' fluisterde ik terug, niet goed wetend wat ik verder moest zeggen.

'Ja, kijk maar.'

Ik boog me haar kant op en kon nu inderdaad zien dat één van de mannen een bladzijde van het album omsloeg en iets wat op een plattegrond leek uitvouwde.

'Ons oude huis in Semarang!' riep hij.

'Oh, Semarang,' lachte de vrouw naast mij, 'Ken je Semarang?' vroeg ze me.

'Vanuit de boeken,' zei ik, 'maar ik ben er nog nooit geweest. Ik ga er binnenkort naartoe.'

'O wat leuk. Semarang is een mooie stad hoor.'

Mijn plan was inderdaad om naar Semarang te gaan in verband met mijn onderzoek naar koloniale woningen en woon-cultuur in de laat koloniale periode. Semarang was de eerste gemeente van Nederlands-Indië die in de jaren '10 van de vorige eeuw grootschalige stedelijke uitbreidingsplannen maakte

diseases. The new developments contrasted with the simple living conditions, often viewed as unhygienic, of the Javanese in their kampongs, which lacked sanitary facilities. Well-equipped bathrooms are shown next to pits in the ground that served as toilets, and sleek European-style dwellings next to bamboo huts. According to these publications, the European home had become the frontline in a cultural and moral battle within the colony, with the dazzling and clinical *whiteness* of the Dutch colonial living environment in the Indies—white clothing, white sheets, white kitchens and bathrooms, white houses—deployed as a weapon.

I stood up and approached the three elderly men to look at the floor plan spread out on the table.

'Good afternoon,' I began. 'Sorry to interrupt, but I heard you talking about a house in Semarang, and that aroused my interest.' They turned to look at me with surprise. 'Umm, you see, I'm an architecture historian,' I added, 'and my subject is colonial architecture. Would you mind if I examined the book with you?'

'Really? How interesting. Why yes, of course. Perhaps you might be able to tell us a thing or two.' The men laughed, pleased with this sudden interest in their brief *tour de memoires*.

'Who knows,' I smiled, and introduced myself.

As I didn't feel any desire to dominate the conversation, I asked them about the house shown on the floor plan. The man who had just unfolded the plan—I would know him thereon as Mr Henri—turned a few pages of the album and showed me a photograph of a young family seated around a small table in what was still a bare-looking garden in front of a newly built house.

'That's me,' said Henri as he smiled and pointed to a young boy of around ten, standing proudly beside a young woman, his left hand resting on her shoulder. 'We lived in that house until the war.' He turned back to the floor plan and now spoke to the other men.

'Our house was suitably oriented, receiving morning sunshine on the rear gallery with the front facing West. It was

en voorzag in publieke woningbouwprojecten. In publicaties uit die tijd van onder andere H.F. Tillema, een bevlogen apotheker, entrepreneur, amateur fotograaf en lobbyist voor betere hygiënische omstandigheden in de kolonie, trof ik plannen en talloze foto's van deze nieuwbouwprojecten, begeleid door statistische gegevens die sterftecijfers als gevolg van epidemieën en infectieziekten in kaart brachten, en in contrast gebracht met de eenvoudige, vaak als onhygiënisch bestempelde leefomgevingen van de Javanen in de kampongs, waar sanitaire voorzieningen ontbraken. Goed uitgeruste badkamers staan afgebeeld naast kuilen in de grond die als toilet diende, en strakke, in Europese stijl gebouwde woningen, naast doorgezakte bamboe hutten. De Europese woning leek in deze publicaties wel de frontlinie geworden van een culturele en morele strijd binnen het koloniale gebied, waarbij het verblindende en klinische wit dat de leefwereld van de Nederlander in Indië kenmerkte (witte kleding, witte lakens, witte keukens en badkamers, witte huizen) werd ingezet als wapen.

Ik stond op en liep naar de drie oude mannen om mee te kijken naar de plattegrond die op tafel lag.

'Goedemiddag,' zei ik, 'sorry dat ik stoor, maar ik hoorde jullie spreken over een woning in Semarang, en dat interesseert me wel.' Ik werd met een verbaasde blik aangekeken. 'Euhhh ja, ik ben architectuurhistoricus, ziet u,' vervolgde ik snel 'en ik houd me bezig met koloniale architectuur. Zou ik misschien mogen meekijken?'

'Zo, zo... interessant, ja natuurlijk. Misschien dat je ons dan nog het een en ander kan vertellen.' De mannen lachte, ingenomen met deze plotse aandacht voor hun kleine *tour de memoires*.

'Wie weet,' lachte ik vriendelijk en stelde me voor.

Omdat ik niet zo'n behoefte voelde om zelf het woord te nemen vroeg ik naar het huis dat op de plattegrond stond afgebeeld. De man—later zou ik hem leren kennen als meneer Henri—die daarjuist de plattegrond had uitgevouwen, sloeg enkele pagina's van het album om en liet een foto zien van een

pleasant to sit in the front gallery in the morning because it provided some shadow. My mother occupied herself there with
pots, plants and flowerbeds. During the afternoon the warm sun
turned away from the cosy rear gallery, so it was not too warm
in the late afternoon.'

Henri's fingers moved across the drawing on the page, as
though the very act of touching the various spaces revived
the memories of the house in his mind. I could now see that it was
the floor plan of a 'linked house'. Written in the bottom-right
corner was *'Housing Association Semarang, 1920'*. His finger
paused on the space labelled as the "front gallery".

'Our front gallery was not lavishly furnished,' he went on.
'We had an oval table made of marble, with half a dozen rocking
chairs and two large palms in ornately decorated Japanese
flowerpots. Suspended above the table was a chandelier. If my
father did not have to leave early, he would linger in his morning gown for a while in the front gallery, where he drank his coffee,
smoked a cigar, and read the post.'

One of the other men joined in enthusiastically: 'My mother
always said, "Theo, remember that the first thing the domestic
servant must do early in the morning is open up the windows
in the front and rear galleries!" In the evening everything was kept
shut, both to discourage thieves and riffraff and to benefit our
health, thus from a hygiene point of view.'

'Because of the humidity?' I asked.

'Exactly,' Theo continued. 'Damp conditions in marshy
areas or near wide and shallow rivers and lakes meant that people could catch a fever before even realizing it. After all the
windows had been opened in the morning, the servants then had
to dust all the furniture. Routine morning chores. Every day
everything was covered in a layer of dust that entered through the
open windows or between the louvres.'

'My parents received guests in the front gallery,' said the
third man, whose name I unfortunately cannot recall, 'but our
family were usually to be found in the rear gallery, especially during the day. That's where meals were taken.'

jong gezin dat rond een tafeltje zat in een nog wat kale tuin voor een nieuw opgeleverde woning.

'Dat ben ik,' zei Henri lachend, wijzend naar een jongen van een jaar of tien die trots naast een jonge vrouw stond, zijn linkerhand op haar schouder rustend. 'In dat huis hebben we tot de oorlog gewoond.' Hij haalde opnieuw de plattegrond tevoorschijn zich nu tot de andere mannen wendend.

'Ons huis was goed georiënteerd, het kreeg de morgenzon aan de achtergalerij. Dus de voorkant lag naar het Westen. 's Morgens vroeg was het aangenaam in de voorgalerij zitten, die dan enigszins beschaduwd was. Mijn moeder hield zich daar met de bloemen, potten en perken bezig. De warme middag zon draaide gedurende de dag weg van de gezellige achtergalerij zodat het daar in de namiddag niet te warm was.'

Henri liet nu zijn vingers over tekening glijden, alsof het aanraken van de verschillende ruimtes de herinneringen aan het huis weer in hem naar boven haalde. Ik kon nu zien dat het een plattegrond van een 'gekoppelde woning' was, rechts onderin stond geschreven 'Woningvereeniging Semarang, 1920'. Hij liet zijn vinger rusten bij de ruimte die stond aangeduid als "voorgalerij".

'De voorgalerij was bij ons niet overdadig gemeubileerd,' vertelde hij verder. We hadden er een ovale marmeren tafel staan, met een zestal wipstoelen en twee grote palmen in sierlijk bewerkte Japanse bloempotten. Er hing een kroonlamp boven de tafel. Als mijn vader er niet vroeg op uit moest, bleef hij altijd nog even in zijn morgen-toilet in de voorgalerij zitten, waar hij dan zijn koffie gebruikte, zijn sigaar rookte, en de post las.'

Een van de andere mannen reageerde enthousiast: 'Mijn moeder zei altijd, "Theo, onthoudt dat het eerste wat de huis-bediende in de vroege morgen moet doen, is de vensters van de voor- en binnengalerij openzetten!" 's Avonds werd alles afgesloten, zowel ter wering van dieven en gespuis als ter bevorder-ing der gezondheid, dus vanuit een hygiënisch oogpunt.'

'Vanwege het vocht?' vroeg ik.

'Precies ja,' vervolgde Theo, 'een vochtige dampkring, bij moerassige plaatsen of bij grote ondiepe rivieren en plassen,

'Next to the front gallery we had a side room,' said Henri, slowly sliding his finger across the plan from room to room, 'which overlooked the street; that was my mother's workroom, where she kept her sewing machine. From there you entered my bedroom, which in turn led to my parents' bedroom.'

'Oh yes, ...' interjected the woman who had been sitting at the table next to mine. By now she had joined us, introducing herself as Caat and chuckling. 'Did the window drapes match the patterns on the bed curtains?'

Henri shrugged his shoulders. 'I don't remember exactly, but there was a big crib covered with a *klamboe* to keep out the mosquitos. My mother always hung a damp hand-towel on her wash basin rack as a kind of diversion. It proved effective in attracting mosquitos.'
I let my gaze roam across the rather abstract lines of the floor plan, and in the sequence of rooms I suddenly noticed that beside the main house there was a kind of outbuilding containing—I read—the water closet, bathroom, kitchen, pantry and servant quarters.

'Did you all have servants?' I asked, pointing to the outbuilding on the floor plan, adding that I wondered why these spaces were separated from the rest of the house.

'Oh sure, outbuildings,' answered Theo. 'We also had them. Indeed, they were mostly used by the native servants. Larger houses usually had outbuildings behind the main building on both sides, stretching back to the rear of the site. A pavilion consisting of one or sometimes two interconnected rooms, arranged in a row and, next to them, a series of spaces—pantries, kitchens, servant rooms, bathrooms, stables/garages, toilets and so on.'

'Those with sufficient resources were not sparing in their number of servants,' continued the third man. 'Each servant performed a particular duty, for which he alone was responsible. The consequence was that one or two servants simply would not suffice. In households with a limited number of servants, some duties were combined. In cases where the number of servants employed by the house was limited to four, they consisted of a cook, *baboe*, houseboy and gardener.'

maakte dat mensen ongemerkt de sluipkoorts konden krijgen. Nadat alle vensters in de ochtend weer open waren gezet, moesten de bedienden al het meubilair afstoffen. De gewone kleine dagelijkse morgenbezigheden. Alles raakte natuurlijk dagelijks met een laagje stof bedekt, omdat het stof van overal, door de geopende vensters of tussen de neergelaten jaloezieën, door kon binnendringen.'

'Mijn ouders ontvingen hun gasten in de voorgalerij,' zei de derde man, wiens naam ik helaas vergeten ben, 'maar als gezin waren we het meest in de achtergalerij te vinden, vooral overdag. Daar werden ook de maaltijden gebruikt.'

'Wij hadden naast de voorgalerij een zijkamer,' Henri verschoof zijn vinger langzaam over de plattegrond van kamer naar kamer, 'die op straat uitzag, daar had mijn moeder haar werkkamer. Er stond een naaimachine. Via die kamer kon je mijn slaapkamer binnengaan die op haar beurt weer verbonden was met de slaapkamer van mijn ouders.'

'Och ja, ...' de mevrouw die naast me aan het tafeltje had gezeten was er inmiddels ook bij komen staan. Ze stelde zich voor als Caat en grinnikte. 'Waren de venstervitrages in overeenstemmende patronen met die van de bedgordijnen?'

Henri haalde zijn schouders op. 'Dat weet ik niet precies meer maar er stond een groot ledikant met een *klamboe* om muskieten tegen te gaan. Mijn moeder legde altijd een natte half uitgewrongen handdoek aan haar wastafelrekje, een soort afleidingsmanoeuvre, daar kwamen de muskieten gretig op af.'

Ik liet mijn ogen over de wat abstracte lijnen van de plattegrond glijden en in de aaneenschakeling van vertrekken viel me toen plots op dat naast de hoofdwoning een soort klein bijgebouwtje getekend was, waar, zo las ik, de w.c., de badkamer, de keuken, de provisiekamer en de bediendenvertrekken gesitueerd werden.

'Hadden jullie allemaal bedienden?' vroeg ik. Ik wees naar het bijgebouwtje op de plattegrond en zei dat ik me afvroeg waarom deze ruimtes van de rest van het huis gescheiden waren.

'Ah ja de bijgebouwen,' zei Theo 'die hadden wij ook. Ze waren grotendeels voor de inlandsche bedienden bestemd,

'Oh yes, the *baboe*. I had a number of those,' said Caat as she grasped my arm. 'The *baboe* will go to great lengths, I sometimes heard mothers saying to one another, to be nice and gentle with the tender child, only to then... *ruin it*.'

Surprised at this comment, I withdrew my arm. 'How do you mean exactly?'

Raising a cautionary finger, she explained how mothers could never let their child notice that things were getting too much or too difficult for them, even if they were tired or suffering from a migraine. 'Don't snap angrily at the child. Petulance like that is grist to the mill of the *baboe*.' Caat, carried away by the memories that came flooding back, set the scene for us "'Jo, nonnie, mama marah," whispers the aggrieved child—"Mama is angry"—as she is being dismissed, and the rift, the first between mother and child, is subtly opened. And the notion of a figure to be feared and avoided settles in that young and impressionable mind for years. *Baboe* then picks up the child, carries her away in the shawl, in the native manner of course, which you should never allow, and disappears with them to the servant quarters. That was, so to speak, an example of poor parenting, because it provoked dishonesty, insincerity, deceit and other unpleasant native qualities.'

Caat pulled a chair towards her and sat down with a sigh. She bowed her head wearily, as though contemplating the scene she had just performed. The men, meanwhile, had started discussing the kitchen.

'The kitchen, yes. A large, blackened, smoky, dim space. I recall that the newly fashioned officers' homes had respectable kitchens, designed as much as possible in the European style. Nonetheless, they soon acquired an Indies stamp, because they were staffed by native female servants who tried to alter everything to suit their own tastes. They didn't feel comfortable in pristine surroundings. So the annual cleaning involved giving the walls three coats of white paint!'

'But a skilful cook made good use of her hands and could put even the most capable Dutch kitchen maid to shame. Working nimbly, they possess the talent to prepare a variety of meals. Even the most ill-disposed individuals felt a pang of hunger as soon as they smelled the cooking. No exaggeration!'

ja. Grotere huizen hadden vaak aan weerszijden achter het hoofdgebouw, naar het achtererf uitgestrekte bijgebouwen: een paviljoen, bestaande uit één, soms twee in elkaar lopende vertrekken, achter elkaar gelegen en, daarachter, doorlopende reeksen kamers bestaande uit provisiekamers, een keuken, bediendenkamers, badkamers, stallen/garages, toiletten, enz.'

'Zij die het konden, bekrompen zich niet op het aantal bedienden,' vervolgde de derde man, 'elke bediende had zijn vast werk waarvoor hij zich dus alleen ook aansprakelijk stelde. Dit had tot gevolg dat men in den regel niet met een of twee bedienden voor alles kon volstaan. In huishoudens, waar men slechts een gering aantal bedienden had, werden wel enige dienstverrichtingen gecombineerd. Wanneer men dan slechts vier bedienden erop na kon houden, werd er een kokkie, een baboe, een bediende (jongen) en een tuinman genomen.'

'Och ja, de baboe, die heb ik er verschillende gehad,' zei Caat, terwijl ze mijn arm vastpakte. 'De baboe zal zich uitsloven, hoorde ik enkele moeders wel eens tegen elkaar zeggen, om goed en lief voor het tedere kindje te zijn, en om het te... *bederven*.'

Ik trok verbaasd mijn arm terug. 'Hoe bedoelt u precies?'

Ze vertelde, terwijl ze waarschuwend een vinger opstak, hoe moeders nooit hun kind, zelfs als ze moe waren of hoofdpijn hadden, mochten laten merken dat het hen te veel of te lastig was. 'Snauw het kind niet af in een gemene bui. Juist zulke kregele buien zijn koren op de molen van de baboe.' Caat, meegesleept door haar opborrelende herinneringen, ensceneerde nu de situatie: '"jo, nonnie, mama marah", sust het pruilend kindje, dat wordt weggezonden en ... de kloof, de eerste tussen moeder en kind, is behendig gegraven. "Mama is boos," is gezegd en in dat jonge hoofdje, zo ontvankelijk voor indrukken, zetelt voor lange jaren de gedachte aan een wezen, dat ontzien en gevreesd moet worden. Baboe neemt dan het kind op, draagt het in de *slendang* weg, (natuurlijk op de inlandse wijze), hetgeen je nooit moet toelaten en verdwijnt er mee naar de bediendenkamers. Dat was, zogezegd, een slechte opvoeding, een die oneerlijkheid, onoprechtheid, bedrog en andere lelijke (Indische) eigenschappen aankweekte.'

'And next to the kitchen was the *goedang*, or pantry. Always trouble with vermin. White ants, for example, tiny yellowish-white insects that looked a little fleshy. One time we had them in the house, under the bed, in closets, in the *goedang*, beneath crates. The servants set a few chickens loose and they eagerly pecked up the fat little creatures. White ants apparently live together in colonies, with a queen at the helm. Only by catching her, it was said, could the colony be disbanded.'

'On occasion, a servant would steal something from the *goedang*—a herring from a newly opened barrel, or a few salted eggs or something like that.'

'The bathroom and water closet were often to be found in the outbuildings too. In the bathroom there was a tub made entirely of Portland cement, 80 centimetres high, for the bathwater.'

'Yes, quite right, and outside there were usually two pits. The one with the best water was intended for household use (for the kitchen, especially potable water); the other, not as clean, for bathwater and the washing needs of servants. The first pit was covered.'

The conversation was still ringing around my mind on the train back to Brussels. After studying the floor plan, the men began talking about the pictures in the album again. They were so absorbed in their reminiscing that they scarcely noticed that I'd taken my leave and departed quietly. After a lengthy search I came across a floor plan of a 'linked house', large in size, designed by the '*Semarang Housing Association*', (1920), in a book from 1931 that chronicled Semarang. I decided to make a model of it to record my remarkable encounter with Caat and the three gentlemen, thereby lending physical form to their descriptions of home life in the Dutch East Indies.

The conversation in this text is composed of sentences taken from the handbook *Ons Huis in Indië* by Mrs J.M.J. Catenius-van der Meijden, Semarang, 1908. In this handbook, which was addressed to Dutch housewives in the Dutch East Indies, Catenius-van der Meijden explains in detail how to live in the colony and how to run a household.

Caat trok een stoel naar zich toe en zette zich met een zucht neer. Ze boog vermoeid het hoofd, alsof ze haar zojuist gespeelde spel overdacht. Ondertussen discussieerde de oude mannen over de keuken.

'De keuken ja, dat was een ruime, maar zwart uitziende, rokerige, donkere ruimte. Ik weet nog dat die nieuwerwetse officierswoningen nette keukens hadden, zoveel mogelijk op Europese leest geschoeid; toch kregen ze dikwijls spoedig het Indische cachet, doordat er inlandse vrouwelijke bedienden in werkten die alles zoveel mogelijk naar hun hand trachtten te zetten. Zij vonden het onbehagelijk in zo'n fris paleis. De keuken kreeg dan ook bij de jaarlijkse schoonmaak en bij het witten van de muren een driedubbele beurt!'

'Maar, een handige kokkie stond nooit met de handen verkeerd en maakte de knapste Hollandse keukenmeid te schande. Ze konden vlug en prompt werken, en hadden het talent om uiteenlopende spijzen te bereiden. Zelfs de meest afkerige mensen deed het watertanden, zodra men iets van die etensluchten opving, ik overdrijf niet!'

'En naast de keuken was de goedang, het provisiehok. Altijd gedoe met ongedierte. Witte mieren bijvoorbeeld, kleine geelwitte diertjes die er als het ware vettig uitzien. Die hadden we een keer in huis, onder een bed, in kasten, in de goedang, onder kisten. De bedienden lieten er dan een paar kippen op los die gretig de vette diertjes oppikten. De witte mieren huizen schijnbaar bij elkaar in koloniën, met een koningin aan het hoofd. Alleen door deze te vangen, wordt beweerd, lost zich de kolonie op.'

'Er werd ook wel eens wat door bedienden uit de goedang gestolen. Een haring uit het pas opengemaakte tonnetje, dan wel een paar gezouten eieren of iets van dien aard.'

'De badkamer en w.c. zaten ook vaak in het bijgebouw. In de badkamer stond een geheel uit portland cement gebouwde gepleisterde bak, iets van 80 cm hoog, voor het badwater.'

'Ja, klopt, en buiten waren gewoonlijk twee putten, waarvan die met het beste water voor huiselijk gebruik (keuken,

drinkwater) bestemd was, de andere, minder goede, voor badwater en bediendengeplas. De eerste put werd overdekt.'

Eenmaal, terug in de trein naar Brussel gonsde de gesprekken nog na in mijn hoofd. De mannen hadden na het bestuderen van de plattengrond hun gesprek over de foto's in het album voortgezet. Ze gingen zo op in hun herinneringen, dat ze nauwelijks opmerkte dat ik hen gedag zei en stilletjes vertrok. Na lang zoeken vond ik in het gedenkboek van Semarang uit 1931 een plattegrond van een gekoppelde woning, groot type, ontworpen door *Woningvereeniging 'Semarang',* (1920). Ik besloot hiervan een maquette te maken om de opmerkelijke ontmoeting met Caat en de drie mannen vast te leggen en de beschrijvingen van hun huis in Indië te verruimtelijken.

Het gesprek in deze tekst is opgebouwd uit zinnen afkomstig van het handboek *Ons Huis in Indië* van mevrouw J.M.J. Catenius-van der Meijden, Semarang, 1908. In dit handboek, dat gericht was aan Nederlandse huisvrouwen in Nederlands-Indië, legt Catenius-van der Meijden in detail uit hoe er in de kolonie gewoond en geleefd diende te worden en hoe een huishouden gerund moest worden.

The Body as

Witness

Listen to the sensitive, they are the future

SOERIA VAN DEN WIJNGAARD

The three core human desires are simple. To be seen, to be heard, and to be loved for who we are, including who we are becoming. Yet, three of the most urgent and complex problems within our contemporary societies: alienation, lack of sustainability and inequality, together form counterweights to these desires, and prevent them from being met. What is notable is that the three desires have a clear commonality: attention, and attention is the ingredient that differentiates our *hearing* from our *listening*.

Issues arise when we can't, or choose not to, meet our desires in the long-term. We instead chase ideals that seem or 'are' more important to us. Contemporary society is designed around the 'hit' that fills our internal void and keeps (amongst other things) capitalism functioning. The internalized hurt within us, the internal criticus and its needs scream to be met to control its immense aversion to the 'mistakes' we make daily.

The main consequence of this codependency (read: addiction) is a loss of intuition and therefore of resilience. Through denial, active disowning, and rejection of our experiences, we are taught to let our *nurture* overpower our *nature*. We stop listening internally as we place our power elsewhere. We stop trusting our own rhythms and the pinches in our bodies. We view neurodiversity as something unworthy of celebration, leading to hostility towards others because their "otherness" threatens our illusionary sense of safety, based on a false and fixed sense of self.

A result of this is that mass consciousness and bodies of humanity are dominated by fear. Nervous systems mostly operate from the parasympathetic state: alert and ready to fight or take flight, or worse: freeze, making it impossible to listen deeply and respond beyond the surface. The unconscious addiction to action alienates us from one another, and also from ourselves. On a global scale this creates an un-sustainable, unjust world.

With the resurgence of feminine energy[1]—or, more simply put: the dormant desire in all bodies to reconnect with the planet, our nature, the body, and it's under-explored senses, we inevitably face complex relationship dynamics. We grow in awareness of what we don't want and continue to walk paths less travelled, such as communal parenthood, polyamorous relationships, dual citizenship, and other choices that celebrate presupposed complexity and therefore, counter 'efficiency culture'. As our culture progresses back to living interdependently, we are forced to re-learn to exist within structures of collaboration, meaning that we don't always get what we (think we) want. With independence comes the necessary growth of self-responsibility: noticing and handling inner volatility and communicating what one needs when one needs it. For such communication to take place, one must be safe to listen to oneself and others in the moment, and not years afterwards. This is a huge venture. However, in doing so, we develop our listening in the broadest sense possible; internally and externally. The archetype for this is the witness. It is instantaneous and creates far more objective observations due to its sharp sense of context. This form of awareness within you is always present, yet easily forgotten. An awareness that doesn't judge or act but simply receives and observes. It cannot exist on its own, but we need to listen to it more. I believe the sensitive, the neurodivergent and the conscious creators[2] hold the potential to lead in their ability to both embody and create from the witness archetype because they are *trained perceivers* and often possess a high sensitivity trait. They strive to present radical ideas in relatively safe spaces and to live their life as the embodiment of these same ideas.

Neighbor in Ikaria, Greece. 2018.
Taken on analogue film by Soeria

How can we learn to actively witness? The first step is to relax the nervous system, come back to the breath and slowly extend to the other senses. Many routes to safely experiencing the body in public space are available. Through, for example, mindful and gentle movements, exposure to the cold and humming, singing and laughter, the longest nerve in the body is stimulated and, consequently, mind and body relax.[3] Creatives are often born with high sensitivity traits.[4] They are the people who, almost without thinking, change the lights in the room, open the windows and adjust the temperature. Only some are aware that they do this to make sure those present around them feel more comfortable. Highly sensitive people (about 15–20% of the population, among all genders, races, and countries) sub- or consciously develop into trained facilitators for manipulation of environments, and therefore are specialized as 'alterers of mental and physical states.' Sensing *more* naturally requires strategies to not become over-stimulated in 'normal' situations. These primordial strategies start with the somatic; through consciously sensing the body one can learn what to do, quickly. For example, if you notice that your vision becomes blurry then turn the music down, focus on the breath or leave. A rich-inner world in combination with sensorial training will make one very aware of stimuli and therefore better able to curate an experience for themselves, or someone else in turn, that is attuned to their sensory needs.

Singer & friend Luca Warmer floating in the sea in Sparta, Greece. 2018. Taken on analogue film by Soeria

Through the experience of art, we become active witnesses. Art and sound can help grow our capabilities to both feel and give meaning to inner volatility through the exposure to ranges and spectra of emotions, sensations, and thoughts. Radical ideas are presented by artists in innumerable ways and through a multitude of media. These ideas, presented in a curated space will, over time and exposure, more likely be accepted by the body and mind through the workings of the nervous system. With the rise of sensorial art, ideas are experienced in an even more volatile way. You could call this the embodiment of ideas, whilst others may call it history or science. Either way, through art and sound, an idea has been given a tangible or visible form and the ways in which these ideas are translated, expressed, and are related to, can speak volumes. Which leads to the question, are our thoughts, physical sensations, and supernatural events part of an artwork? Absolutely. Being exposed to a work of sound, or a work of art, reveals unique subtleties that inform our progression instantly.

From our willingness to listen we can also expand our emotional depth. Art and sound help to inform our progression in the way we adjust our behaviours to the work itself and each other whilst we are around it in public areas.

The five layers of listening, drawing by Soeria, theory by Oscar Timboli.

meaning

unsaid

context

content

yourself

During such an experience, one might change perspective, or deepen their understanding of a certain perception or sensation. Art and sound are translations of radical ideas, and the reception of these ideas enhances connection. A pleasant collective experience creates togetherness; once we pass the threshold, shared sensorial experiences open opportunities for intimacy. These can happen at multiple moments during an experience. For example: *Before* the experience, through the ritual of becoming open to the notion of experiencing. *During the experience*: being open and experiencing, and experiencing yourself experiencing, and *afterwards*: in digesting and sharing. This is an embodied, or felt intimacy, an intimate communication in which ineffable sensations are often delicately shared. Curated experiences create a form of communication that, as a by-product, enhances active perceiving and in doing so, increases one's emotional depth. The after-effect of an experience is hard to measure, but the lingering effects of being exposed to something radical in a safe space enhances intra- and inter-personal connection, bypassing the mind as the most important force. Art and sound therefore enhance our depth, whether we enjoyed the experience or not.

Sound artist Pauline Oliveros emphasized psychological growth in her work, alongside the three core desires: to be seen, to be heard and to be loved in all forms of being. Pauline was queer, deviant, stunning. Through her life and work, she used her 'otherness' to change both the male-dominated electro-acoustic, experimental music scene in New York in the 70's, as well as using her power as a composer to let others experience what it means to listen deeply, inclusively, and queerly.[5] Towards the end of her life, she worked with city engineers in New York, showing them that city design should take acoustics into consideration to enhance quality of life. This was particularly notable in the proposed reduction of noise pollution so that pedestrians could be aware of sounds that are necessary for their safety, and so they could have the ability to engage in conversation or hear themselves think whilst in public space.

Oliveros' work helped us to understand that we hear with our ears but listen with our whole being. What we listen to consists of multiple layers of content, context, the unsaid, and meaning. It is impossible to deny the subjectivity of our listening. Oliveros' concept of the sonosphere embraces the full "sweep and barrage of energies both within and surrounding the body, including the magnetic, electrical, electromagnetic, geomagnetic, and quantum, as well as the acoustical. It resonates among personal and interpersonal, musical, earth, and cosmological scales formed by physics and metaphysics.".[6] She came to this theory by practicing Qigong which, for her, entailed experiencing listening with the palms of her hands to sense electromagnetic fields. By delving deeper and deeper into the layers of meaning and embodiment surrounding sound, Oliveros' corporeal practices challenge, still to this day, Western conceptions of self.[7]

Three listeners in Soeria's installation Witness What Remains: to Listen is to Love (2018-2020) Taken on analogue film by Floris Meijer.

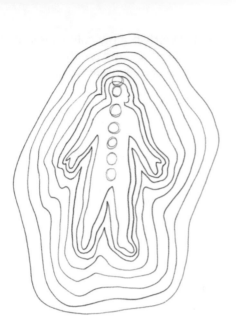

A simplified drawing of the seven layers of the auric field around a human body.

In my experience, sound and art create entry points that lead us to parts of ourselves we didn't know existed or that oppose one another. Throughout my own research I've worked with the activation of memories that are passively stored but can be brought back up through sound stories. Associative states can enhance mind travel along memory chains that seem to be randomly connected. Regardless of how unclear these experiences were for my listeners, they felt like they had travelled far, sometimes back into their own memory, and many mentioned feelings of deep relaxation in the process. The after-effect of associative experience enhances the perception of daily life. This is where the magic occurs.

     My practice as a creative, a yoga teacher, a workshop facilitator and, more recently, of dealing with physical illness, are inseparably intertwined with my own experiences with Pauline Oliveros' work. My installation 'Witness What Remains', shown as part of the *Rights of Way* exhibition, offered a space in which one could experience authentic listening through the physical interaction (playing!) with +/- 300 small ceramic bells. The fragility and non-linearity of the installation invited the practice of refraining from acting or listening on autopilot. Actively using the physical space of the 'white cube' and the feelings it can produce doesn't feel safe yet for many. Arguably, it may never be entirely the right space for this kind of work, but my colleagues and I are very happy to address side-effects around touch, safety and play and will continue to offer layered experiences in unexpected places.

Returning and cultivating the inner witness helps us to navigate not only the interpersonal consequences of injustice, inertia, and inauthenticity, but also to address colonisation of mind and body. Reclaiming sensual and subjective experience helps reveal the spaces in which we are not free.[8] Privilege comes with responsibilities to work on oneself, for those who came before us and for those who will come after us. The conscious mending of incongruences between one's inner and outer self through the act of witnessing.

Pauline worked with a 'focal' focus, which in my work, 'Witness What Remains', is literally a sounding point, a bell, activated by physical touch. Next to the focal focus, she worked with a 'global' focus, meaning that the focus is on expanding one's 'area' of listening both inwards and outwards. The intention of deep listening is to become aware of both the inside and outside. The practice intends to heighten and expand consciousness of sound in the broadest definition possible. Pauline spent long periods of time noticing her own listening and discerning its effects, and so listened deeply to her body-mind continuum.[9] She also discerned between two forms: focal attention and global attention. If one is focused on an exclusive stream of sounds, such as a speech, all energy must be focused on that one stream to follow what is being transmuted. In doing so one must keep renewing their attention. Through this form of awareness, one is likely to be disconnected from parts of the self and the environment one is in. Global attention is expanding this listening to focus outwards, taking in and listening to everything that is around and inside of you. Pauline also called this inclusive listening. "In order to do what I call Deep Listening we have to include everything".[10] It may take a while to understand and become familiarised with this method of listening. I recommend starting with sensing resistance in the body. Resistance shows up differently in each body but tends to have similar somatic habits. It can be recognized through the nature of the sensation itself or because of the clear location in the body where the uncomfortable sensation is occurring. Energy in motion or emotion, when listened to with one's full attention, fades quicker than the mind screams.

In 2017, writer Hanzi Freinacht presented The Listening Society,[11] a model of welfare that focused on the development of depth in all citizens. He writes, "as a society, we haven't fully admitted to ourselves and to one another just how sensitive, how utterly emotionally vulnerable, we really are. The aim here is to make this embarrassing truth publicly obvious, so that we can together reshape society thereafter—until even the most sensitive among us can blossom, until the truly sensitive become our kings and queens".[12] To do so, we must see listening and acting upon our truths as a practice that is ever evolving and expanding, and learn to listen deeply, internally, and externally as much as possible, and to not get lost in convenient, yet superficial, external acceptance. This is not a call to celebrate individualism, as we need to celebrate both dependence and independence to grow into interdependence. We needn't agree always. Yet, sometimes we do agree, after we pass through resistance. And the neurodivergent are often those who notice first.

We must listen to the sensitive, as they are the future.

Percussion is a method of tapping on a body's surface to determine the underlying structures and is used in medical examinations.drawing by Soeria

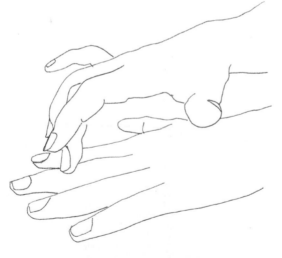

[1]
'The feminine' is an energy that is the opposite of, yet not separate to, masculine energy. Both polarities are not restricted to these binaries. I understand it as more fluid. Each human consists of a dynamic and unique combination of both energies. In Taoism, Yoga and Shamanism this is described as Yīn and Yang (or Alpha and Omega) energy; unable to exist separately. Throughout more recent history the feminine has been repressed. We can find this back in the Goddess Lilith archetype that led to feminine (over-)expression (phrase two) and is now transforming into harmony (phase 3) in which the masculine and feminine both exist simultaneously. I identify as a cis-woman and was raised in an esoteric community and environment that led to exploration of these concepts. I have been immersed in the practice of yoga for 8 years, obtained a yoga teacher training and reiki. I train and joyfully participate in women's healing circles among many other practices. Further reading for the topic includes Noble, V. (1991). Shakti Woman: Feeling Our Fire, Healing Our World—The New Female Shamanism (1st ed.). Harper San Francisco. Estés, C. P. (1996). Women Who Run with the Wolves: Myths and Stories of the Wild Woman Archetype (Reissue ed.). Ballantine Books. Tzu, L., & Harris, J. (2020). Tao Te Ching: Adapted for the Contemporary Reader. Independently published.

[2]
I include these terms as examples, this list is not exhaustive.

[3]
Gerritsen, R. J. S., & Band, G. P. H. (2018). Breath of Life: The Respiratory Vagal Stimulation Model of Contemplative Activity. Frontiers in Human Neuroscience, 12, 1–15. https://doi.org/10.3389/fnhum.2018.00397

[4]
Aron, E. N., Aron, A., & Jagiellowicz, J. (2012). Sensory Processing Sensitivity. Personality and Social Psychology Review, 16(3), 262–282. https://doi.org/10.1177/1088868311434213

[5]
Oliveros, P. And Don't Call Them "Lady" Composers. (2005). In Software for People (pp. 47–51). Baltimore, USA: Smith P.

[6]
Oliveros, P. (2011). Auralizing in the Sonosphere: A Vocabulary for Inner Sound and Sounding. Journal of Visual Culture, 10(2), 162–168. https://doi.org 10.1177/1470412911402881

[7]
McMullen, T. M. (2010). Subject, Object, Improv: John Cage, Pauline Oliveros, and Eastern (Western) Philosophy in Music. Critical Studies in Improvisation / Études critiques en improvisation, 6(2). https://doi.org/10.21083/csieci.v6i2.851

[8]
"When we say abolish police. We also mean the cop in your head and in your heart". - Tweet by @tourmaliiine, June 8th, 2020.

[9]
Pert, C. B., PhD, & Chopra, D. (1999). Molecules of Emotion The Science Behind Mind Body Medicine (1st edition). New York, USA: Simon & Schuster.

[10]
Wooley, N. (2015). SA7: The Deep Listening Issue. Pauline Oliveros on Deep Listening. Sound American. http://archive.soundamerican.org/sa_archive/sa7/sa7-pauline-oliveros-on-deep-listening.html

[11]
Freinacht, H. (2017). Political metamodernism is the future. In The Listening Society: A Metamodern Guide to Politics Book One (Vol. 1, (p.4)).Copenhagen, Denmark: Metamoderna.

[12]
Freinacht, H. (2017). The Basic Idea. In The Listening Society: A Metamodern Guide to Politics Book One (Vol. 1, (p. 71–72)) Copenhagen, Denmark: Metamoderna.

A Prequel to Critical Walks

ALESSANDRO MARCHI

For the past fifteen years my artist practice has been based on walking. Over the last two years I have formulated a methodology to incorporate statistics and societal critique into my practice. This led to the realisation of a series of public programmes entitled Critical Walks,[1] and to the ongoing process of collecting my thoughts and shared experience in a book format. Whilst working on the book, I took a moment to reflect on my relationship with walking. This text came out of thinking about the meaning of walking in my life, and it is written as if it were a walk in itself, with some unnecessary but inevitable detours. It starts from a childhood memory that meets with an adult's inspiration.

There are two quotes that I keep going back to throughout my work.

One is from the Italian researcher Francesco Careri:

> *"Walking has always generated architecture and landscape, and this practice, all but totally forgotten by architects themselves, has been reactivated by poets, philosophers and artists capable of seeing precisely what is not there, in order to make 'something' be there."*[2]

And one from my father, which you've probably already heard before:

> *"When I was a child I had to walk 5 km everyday to get to school, back and forth, in the mud. You don't know the meaning of the word sacrifice."*

He used to tell me this when I was complaining about something, anything. He was saying how lucky I was that I didn't have to walk to school everyday.[3] As it turns out, the walking back and forth to school, with friends from the adjacent farms, through a little hilly forest, was not that bad. It was a memory that was safe, a place to return to whenever he needed strength. By walking everyday, friendships were made for life.

I struggle to find such memories. As a child, the everyday car commute was making whoever was at the steering wheel stressed and anxious. Everybody was driving on the same road at the same time. It was the 1980s. In Italy every family had two or three cars and FIAT had a huge influence on government policy for mobility.

From my earlier school years I haven't many memories of walking in the city. Although there is one that comes to mind from when my Mom didn't pick me up and I ventured out on the roads on my own. (I think this may have been the only time it happened, but that's probably why it's so memorable). I remember the sense of adventure. From school to my house it was basically a few kilometres, maybe three at max, of straight, heavily trafficked, suburban roads. It was the link between the city center and the main highway, passing through the "industrial zone", the area where car mechanics, prostitutes and tivoli wonderlands coexisted in harmony. I must have been around seven, and my mum found me just before a huge (or maybe not so huge, afterall I was small) traffic crossing. So my adventure actually ended pretty soon after it had begun. I didn't even manage to cross the traffic entanglement which indeed was just a rather small and insignificant small town crossing.

Some decades later I find myself in Oslo, struggling to write about walking and art. I take a detour, which is always something I like to do when walking. If I were to compare my life to a game of chess, my opening strategy has always mostly been about engineering. I studied engineering, I practiced engineering and then made a career out of it. When I was already in the middle game, the stage where you profit off the good choices you made in the opening phase, I drastically changed strategy and swapped engineering for arts. Suddenly, my previously "good" position, where I could play a comfortable and profitable middle game, became an unknown territory where I could lose myself.

During the first year of my new adventure I mainly walked. I was living in Stavanger at that time. A small coastal town in the south west of Norway. I would take a bus until the last stop and then walk back home. Day after day. I was lost and the daily gesture of finding the way home from somewhere in the suburbs would give me a sense of being not quite so lost, perhaps. It would serve both as exercise for the body and lubricant for the thoughts.

I started using walking as a method. One of the strategies within that methodology is to land myself intentionally in an un-known area of the city I had never been before and to find my way home—without GPS, as a way of re-organising my thoughts around the purpose of my life and to feel productive in the new system I found myself in.

Even if banal and mundane and dull, walking long distances in suburban areas defies the imposed order of things. This imposed order of things being very much controlled by the neoliberal agenda where cities are made for you *not* to walk.[4] Instead you should drive your car from your garage to the shopping center, park in the free parking spot and take some electric stairways to the mall. There you can meet other people and everything around is arranged for you to spend money. Then you drive back home, park the car in the garage and from there take the elevator to your flat. From there you can walk to your living room and get lost in your big flat screen television, and you don't even need a field guide to getting lost,[5] the autoplay function at the end of your favourite series does the trick for you.

So what is it that I am doing with walking and art? I think it is a sort of mechanism to strengthen my mental health. According to my experience, walking has been proven an effective method to cope with various minor psychological ailments. I used to walk many hours a day to get tired and ensure that I would sleep better at night.

Combining that with art is my way of coping with anxiety, while hopefully making a living. It is also a way to bypass the lack of good mental healthcare within the free universal care system. It admittedly has its limits and if it works for some it doesn't mean that it works for everybody. And it can also get to a point where it does not serve the same purpose anymore.

For instance, these days I don't walk all that much. Somehow I feel like if I go to walk I need to come up with something to transform the walk into an activity from which to extract an art product, something that allows me to get to know both the surrounding world while finding peace with my inner demons. When I use the term "product" it is because I am aware that the walk itself could already be an art piece, but I always felt the necessity to produce additional objects, as I come from a materialistic background.

This feeling comes after two years of intensely squeezing walking as an art practice. I moved to Oslo in the summer of 2018 to study an MFA and, as I usually do in a new place, I started walking to get to know the place. During a conversation with a new Oslo acquaintance I got to know about a statistical peculiarity present in the map of Oslo. This peculiarity was a gap in life expectancy between adjacent neighbourhoods. A difference of almost ten years within the same city, the kind of difference you would expect to find between different countries. To put it in a global context, a similar difference in life expectancy can be observed between Norway and Bangladesh, the first having 82.3 life expectancy years at birth versus 72.3 of the latter.

On a sunny day during October 2018 I went to exactly where this statistical division stands: between Sagene and Nordre Aker. I got to the Tåsen Allé stop with the 34-bus and I started walking the line of division from there. Walking eastward, the statistical life expectancy was higher on the left side than on the right. While my senses were alert to finding signals and evidence, 20 minutes into the walk, my left ear became clogged and stopped working, affecting my equilibrium. I developed vertigo and had to sit down: my head started hurting a lot and it was impossible to proceed.

The side affected was the one facing the side of the street where the life expectancy is longer. It was like my body felt the imbalance of the human landscape and reflected upon it by shutting one side down as a somatic reaction.

This, to me, is an example of how observations are influenced by how we feel during the process. As my senses became alerted by statistical knowledge, my experience of the walk was in constant relation to the data, as if I was constantly checking whether the hypotheses behind the walk's design were confirmed by the field experience. In fact my body became so imbalanced by the ear's malfunction, that the whole walk became sort of grotesque, transforming a field phenomenological trip into an embodied somatic experience.

What if writing was like walking? Or walking like writing? In order to walk you don't need a destination, you don't even need to agree a priori to a destination, you can just start walking. Nevertheless, each step is a result of a decision process happening more or less consciously. If you are walking in a city, the boardwalks, the zebra crossings, the building and the traffic decide where you are going to walk. Micro turns and deviation from the path can be caused by interactions with other humans.

Here I am, writing lines without a direction, hoping to find one. Isn't this what I have been doing for most of my life? Going in all directions hoping to find one that feels good on my skin? The problem could be that only after a certain period of time things can start to feel good on your skin. We could think about shoes for instance. If one was to judge a pair of good and sturdy, made to last leather shoes, hand made ones with a strong leather sole; if one was to judge them by their first walk, well you would throw them away, they would be painful and hard and horrible. One has to break them in, to endure some pain and blisters for a certain number of walks and kilometers and then something happens and the shoes become comfortable and start to feel like they were made for our feet. But they were never made for our feet. It is due to friction, heat and the modification of our bones in line with the inner part of the shoe that comfort is reached. All of this happens through walking.

I wonder where this metaphor could lead us. In what other parts of our lives can we experience the shoe paradigm? Maybe in a relationship? Maybe in urban development? Maybe when we move to a new city? It is through our movement and use that we change and influence the environment around us. We define the environment around us through our interactions, through the things we buy, through how we treat the people behind the counter, whether we smile or not to our neighbors, and the people we meet whilst walking around our block.

Our environment becomes more and more comfortable as we walk through it, as we experience pain through a series of frictions and conversations.

We grow together. Either apart, in parallel, or really together.

[1]

Critical Walks looks at ways to witness a city on foot, translating statistical data into walkable paths. The central theme is the relationship between the body and statistics in dialogue with urban texture. It is about the consolidation of objective data with subjective observations. It aims at understanding and questioning critical aspects within the city of Oslo, such as immigration, inequality, and ageing through walking experiments and conversations. It is site-based, but it develops a method of investigation that can be re-contextualised in any other city, at any other time.

[2]

Careri, F. (2017). *Walkscapes: Walking as an aesthetic practice.* Culicidae Architectural Press.

[3]

Mostly I was going with a teacher from another class, Leda, who was our neighbor. She drove an old Fiat 500 and we would stop every morning to put some gasoline in the tank, 5000 Lire, the equivalent of 2.5 €.

[4]

Or you are strictly encouraged to walk where there is a walking area already designed for you to do so. This prevents humans from meeting one another in inbetween non commodified spaces. The meetings are managed, somebody else has already decided upon where we can meet a stranger, have an interaction, possibly under a surveillance camera that makes sure the situation is safe.

[5]

Rebecca Solnit, A Field Guide to Getting Lost has been staying with me for a while, though I never finished reading it as every time I got lost into something else.

Blokje Om

CORINNE HEYRMAN

There are countless types of routes.
There is the daily route.
The exact route, also known as the "neurotic walk".
The discovery route.
The functional route.
The far too far route.
The routine route.
The late evening stroll.
The adventurous route.
The elimination route: using walking to get rid of something.
The local route.
The Sunday stroll.
The cold nose route; also called "the knot".
The newsagent route.
The visitor route.
The thoughtful route.
The "I don't want to run, but exercise" route.
The dewy route.
The route outside of a comfort zone.

Choose one of these routes and hit the road.

I, myself, used to prefer 'the exact route'. Always the same block again and again. I was still living in Antwerp at the time, and I had a fixed route along the Scheldt. Through the pedestrian tunnel over the streets of Linkeroever and back again. I knew the city like the back of my hand. I never looked for new routes.

Since I moved back to the Netherlands I have preferred 'the discovery tour'. Every time I walk, I try out new streets, looking at the houses, the front gardens.

I love to go for a walk when it is just getting dark, and families turn on their lights, you can then catch small glimpses of different scenes. I recently saw a man watching television with his Golden Retriever. The dog's head rested on his knee, the flashes of the television screen made it seem very exciting to watch, but they both remained remarkably calm. Once before, I saw three children dancing in a living room. One of them was wearing a Spider-Man costume, all of them wiggling their bottoms back and forth. In the kitchen next door, a man was chopping vegetables on a wooden board. He was bent over the counter as if he was totally absorbed by his leek, or perhaps just thinking about something else. Something that made his head too heavy to bear.

Er zijn talloze soorten ommetjes.
Er is het dagelijkse ommetje.
Het exacte ommetje; ook wel de neurotenwandeling.
Het ontdekkingsommetje.
Het functionele ommetje.
Het veel te verre ommetje.
Het routineuze ommetje.
Het laat-avondommetje.
Het avontuurlijke ommetje.
Het wegwerkommetje; waarbij je het wandelen gebruikt om iets weg te werken.
Het lokale ommetje.
Het zondagsommetje.
Het koude neuzen ommetje; ook wel het knommetje.
Het krantenwinkelommetje.
Het visiteommetje.
Het nadenkommetje.
Het 'Ik wil niet hardlopen wel sporten' ommetje.
Het dauwommetje.
Het ommetje buiten de comfortzone.

Kies één van deze ommetjes uit en ga op pad.

Ikzelf verkoos vroeger 'het exacte ommetje', ook wel de neuroten wandeling. Altijd weer hetzelfde blokje om. Ik woonde toen nog in Antwerpen en ik had een vaste route langs de Schelde door de voetgangerstunnel over de straten van Linkeroever en terug. Ik kende de stad op mijn duimpje. Ik zocht geen nieuwe plekken op. Sinds ik in Nederland woon verkies ik 'het ontdekking- sommetje'. Elke keer weer probeer ik nieuwe straten uit, bekijk de huizen, de voortuinen.

  Ik hou ervan om te wandelen wanneer het net begint te schemeren en de gezinnen hun lampen aan doen. Je kan dan kleine glimpen van verschillende taferelen opvangen, zo zag ik onlangs een man die met zijn Golden Retriever televisie keek. De kop van de hond ruste op zijn knie, door de flitsen van het televisiescherm leek het iets heel spannends waar ze naar keken maar ze bleven er beide opvallend rustig onder. Een keer daarvoor zag ik drie kinderen die in een woonkamer aan het dansen waren. Eén ervan droeg een Spider-Man kostuum, allen wiebelden ze met hun billen heen en weer. In de keuken ernaast hakte een man groenten op een houten plank. Hij stond

These are the small portraits that are behind the windows. *Tableau vivants* of reality, for which I like to walk around the block to see. And when I come across water during my walk, whichever route I have chosen, I always stop for a while. After all, water knows better than humans how to follow time. She knows how to float gently and how you can catch the hard blows of the waves. She knows when to accept something and when to oppose it.

I wish you a good time with your chosen route. That your preference may guide you, but still inspire your sense of adventure.

helemaal over het aanrecht gebogen alsof hij heel erg op ging in zijn prei of juist met zijn gedachten bij iets heel anders was. Iets waarvan zijn hoofd te zwaar werd om te dragen.

Het zijn kleine portretten die zich achter de ramen bevinden. Tableaux vivants van de realiteit, waarvoor ik graag een blokje om loop. En als ik tijdens mijn ommetje water tegenkom, welk ommetje ik ook gekozen heb, dan blijf ik altijd even staan. Het water weet immers beter dan de mens hoe het de tijd volgen moet. Zij weet hoe rustig dobberen gaat en hoe je de harde klappen van de golven kan vangen. Zij weet wanneer je je ergens bij neer moet leggen en wanneer je er juist tegenin moet gaan.

Ik wens je een fijne tijd met je uitgekozen ommetje. Dat je voorkeur leidend mag lijken, maar dat vooral je gevoel voor avontuur het is.

CORINNE
Yes, it is an expression. It is a movement. It's a way to go somewhere.

VOICE-OVER
You may recognize it. That if you stop doing something, or are further away from something...

CORINNE
Yes, it is a kind of breathing of the body

VOICE-OVER
Then you can then better identify what something is. What it means.

CORINNE
Yes, expressive. An expression of your whole body.

VOICE-OVER
For example, since I moved out of my parents' home, I know more about my family. Since I have lived in the Netherlands, I know better how I feel about Belgium.
That's why I asked three people who no longer walk, what walking means to them.

MIEKE
Yes, *freedom.*

VOICE-OVER
I have three discussion partners, including Mieke:

MIEKE
The freedom to say 'Hey, I'm going to do this' or ...

VOICE-OVER
Inge:

CORINNE
Ja, dat is een expressie, dat is een beweging. Dat is een manier om ergens naartoe te gaan.

VOICE-OVER
Misschien herken je het wel. Dat als je met iets stopt of ergens verder van af staat.

CORINNE
Ja, het is een soort ademing van het lichaam.

VOICE-OVER
Dat je dan beter kan benoemen wat iets is. Wat het inhoudt.

CORINNE
Ja, echt een expressieve uitdrukking van je hele lichaam.

VOICE-OVER
Zo weet ik sinds ik uit mijn ouderlijke huis verhuisd ben meer over mijn familie. Sinds ik in Nederland woon, weet ik beter wat ik van België vind. Daarom vroeg ik drie mensen die niet meer lopen wat het voor hen betekent.

MIEKE
Ja, vrijheid.

VOICE-OVER
Ik heb drie gesprekspartners, waaronder MIEKE

MIEKE
De vrijheid om te zeggen 'Hey, ik ga even dit doen' of...

VOICE-OVER
Inge:

INGE
Zeker als mooi weer is, het zonnetje schijnt enzo door de bomen en de blaadjes. Tja, dat was een mooie tijd.

INGE
Especially when the weather is nice, the sun is shining and so, through the trees and leaves.
Oh yes, that was a great time.

VOICE-OVER
And Corinne:

CORINNE
For me not being able to walk is a lack of spontaneity, a lack of sensitivity. Because yes, it also means that your body, or in my case only half, is completely insensitive. You could almost say dead. Making it that your whole body stays very tight. Very, very static.

VOICE-OVER
Corinne was in a car accident in Indonesia, which left her with a spinal cord injury. The lower part of her body is paralysed.

CORINNE
And sometimes you feel like going a little crazy. You feel like jumping. You feel like doing a lot of stretching. You feel like moving your whole body and doing things with it. For a long time, the second part of my body didn't feel like my own at all. You could have taken my legs away, yes, but then I wouldn't have felt it. It is also because during rehabilitation we learn to work with the upper body and regain our strength there, but we do nothing at all with the lower body and I think that is completely wrong.

For example, what I do a lot of now is yoga, I do it on the floor on purpose. I try to do things with my whole body. After doing this, I get the feeling of a whole body. I still can't feel my legs, but I know them better in my mind.

VOICE-OVER
It feels different for Mieke.

MIEKE
I can feel my whole body. I get a response when someone touches my legs. It seems like there are stimuli. I often get spasms. I can

VOICE-OVER
En Corinne:

CORINNE
Voor mij niet kunnen lopen is een gebrek aan spontaniteit, een gebrek aan gevoeligheid. Want ja, het betekent ook dat de helft van jouw lichaam, voor mij alleen de helft, helemaal ongevoelig is. Bijna dood zou je kunnen zeggen. Dat maakt het, dat jouw hele lichaam heel strak blijft. Heel, heel statisch.

VOICE-OVER
Corinne kreeg een auto-ongeluk in Indonesië, waardoor ze een halve dwarslaesie heeft. Het onderste deel van haar lichaam is verlamd

CORINNE
En soms heb je zin om gewoon een beetje gek te worden! Je hebt zin om te springen. Je hebt zin om heel erg te stretchen. Je hebt zin om je hele lichaam te te te bewegen en en dingen daarmee te doen. Een lange tijd voelde het tweede gedeelte van mijn lichaam helemaal niet meer van van mezelf. Je kan sowieso mijn been, ja meenemen. Of ja, ik weet het niet, maar dan voel ik het niet. Het komt ook zo omdat wij tijdens de revalidatie leren om met het bovenlichaam te werken en kracht daar terug te krijgen, maar wij doen dan helemaal niks meer met het benedenlichaam en ik denk dat het helemaal fout is.

Wat ik nu doe is yoga bijvoorbeeld, en ik doe het expres op de grond. En ik probeer om dingen te doen met mijn hele lichaam. Dan krijg ik wel het gevoel van een heel lichaam. Ik kan nog steeds mijn benen niet voelen. Maar ik kan ze meer voelen in mijn hoofd.

VOICE-OVER
Voor Mieke voelt het anders.

MIEKE
Ik voel wel mijn hele lichaam. Ik krijg een reactie als iemand mijn benen aanraakt. Dan lijkt het wel alsof daar, ja prikkels zijn. Dan krijg ik vaak spasmen. Ik voel ook of ik wel of niet goed in bed lig. Het voelt wel als één. Maar soms voelt het ook wel alsof het heel

also feel whether I am lying comfortably in my bed. Then my body feels like one. But sometimes my body also feels like it is very heavy, hanging onto my shoulders.

In this way, I miss walking less than using my arms.

I always dream that I can still do everything. I feel tired when I wake up in the morning because I have done all kinds of things in my dreams at night. You are riding a bike. You drive a car. Waking up is not always pleasant, because then you will be confronted with the situation again. But sometimes it is also nice to dream, then I think '*So, I did that again.*'

VOICE-OVER
Mieke finds freedom in other things

MIEKE
In expressing myself on paper.

VOICE-OVER
She wrote a book with speech technology, and paints with a brush in her mouth.

MIEKE
But also, because I have an electric wheelchair, I can also go outside by myself. I can drive for a while without someone having to be with me. Then you can also be alone for a while. Yes, I like that very much. I have started to look at things differently. I have started to put things into perspective more and I am perhaps more satisfied with the smaller things than someone who runs and flies all day long. Just put me in the sun for ten minutes and I'll be the happiest person in the world.

zwaar is en aan mijn schouders hangt. Ik mis trouwens het lopen minder dan het gebruik van mijn armen.

Ik droom ook altijd dat ik alles nog kan. Moe als ik s 'morgens wakker word, omdat ik s 'nachts in mijn dromen van alles gedaan heb. Je zit op de fiets. Je rijdt auto. Alleen het wakker worden is niet altijd fijn, want dan word je weer geconfronteerd met je situatie. Maar soms is het ook fijn om te dromen, dan denk ik: 'zo dat heb ik toch weer lekker even gedaan.'

VOICE-OVER
Mieke vindt in andere dingen vrijheid

MIEKE
In het jezelf uiten op papier.

VOICE-OVER
Ze schreef met spraaktechnologie een boek, schildert met een penseel in haar mond.

MIEKE
Maar ook doordat ik een elektrische rolstoel heb, kan ik ook zelf naar buiten. Kan ik ook een stukje rijden zonder dat er iemand bij mij moet zijn. Dat je ook eventjes alleen kan zijn. Ja, dat vind ik wel heel fijn. Ik ben anders gaan kijken tegen de dingen aan. Ik denk dat ik meer en beter ben gaan relativeren en misschien met kleinere dingetjes sneller tevreden ben dan iemand die de hele dag loopt te rennen en te vliegen. Zet mij tien minuten in de zon en ben de gelukkigste mens van de wereld.

INGE
Ik ben nu 62 en zo rond mijn... Ik heb altijd al wel een zwakke rug gehad.

INGE
I'm 62 now and I've always had a weak back.

VOICE-OVER
At the age of 60, Inge became a wheelchair-user and has since resided in a residential care centre due to a broken back.

INGE
I came and lived here, and I didn't know anyone at all. I went downstairs and looked around the restaurant. And then I had very strong feeling, really like I was visiting my grandmother.

You come as a young person, and it is so difficult to get to know the fellow residents. And that feeling of: "Yes, but I don't actually belong here yet, because I'm not that old and I don't feel that way yet." But now I've been living here for over two and a half years. You get used to it.

VOICE-OVER
For the first time in her life, Inge is alone.

INGE
Yes, and then you are locked up with yourself and you are confronted by yourself.

VOICE-OVER
Inge spent the past few years indoors.

INGE
And now I watch a lot of television. I have four computer games. Which I really enjoy, so I play them a lot.

In one you can set up aquariums. And then you arrive at different levels,

Inge kwam op haar zestigste met een kapotte rug in een rolstoel en een woonzorgcentrum terecht.

INGE
Ja, dan kom je hier wonen en je kent helemaal niemand. Dan ga je eens naar beneden en je gaat in het restaurant kijken. En toen had ik heel sterk - en ik wil niemand tekort doen, maar echt alsof ik bij mijn oma op bezoek ging.
En dan kom je als jongere, nou ja... Kom je daar ook al heel moeilijk tussen. En dat gevoel van: 'Ja, maar ik hoor hier eigenlijk nog niet, want zo oud ben ik nog niet en zo voel ik me ook nog niet.' Maar nu woon ik hier al dik twee en een half jaar. Je raakt er wel aan gewend.

VOICE-OVER
Voor het eerst in haar leven is Inge alleen.

INGE
Ja en dan zit je eigenlijk ook opgesloten met jezelf en dan word je geconfronteerd met jezelf.

VOICE-OVER
De afgelopen periode bracht Inge binnen door.

INGE
En heel veel televisie kijken. Ik heb nu vier computerspelletjes, waar ik met heel veel plezier dus dat doe ik ook heel veel.
De ene kun je aquariums in gaan richten. En dan kom je in verschillende niveaus aan en krijg je allerlei verschillende landen te zien. En Harry Potter.

and you get to see all kinds of different countries. And there's *Harry Potter*. Also, *Three in a Row*, but that is where all the magic spells are incorporated. And then another where a girl helps her uncle to revive a restaurant and you have to collect points. With those points the girl can create and build new things. And that's great fun too and, what is the fourth again? Oh Willy Wonka! *Willy Wonka and the Chocolate Factory*. Well, this one I really like too. You enter a very empty dark space together with Willy Wonka. And then you start to rebuild his entire fantasy factory step by step. Unbelievable what is in it, the Oompaloompa's and the children who have not kept to agreements, a girl who turns into a large blueberry...

These are the things that you do, so that you can stop yourself and your thoughts for a moment.

VOICE-OVER
She has now learned how to put things into perspective

INGE
Yes, I've been doing this in the two and a half years that I've been here. Because before that, I just had a view of infinite time that went on and on and on and on and on. Because of this feeling, I didn't have time or focus to think at all.

VOICE-OVER
Corinne has since started the foundation EndParalysis to support research into paralysis.

Ook drie op een rij, alle toverspreuken zijn daarin verwerkt. En dan nog een meisje dat haar oom helpt om een restaurant opnieuw, nieuw leven in te blazen en dat je dan punten moet verzamelen. Dat zij dan nieuwe dingen kan neerzetten en opbouwen. En dat is ook heel leuk en wat was de vierde ook weer. Oh Willy Wonka! Willy Wonka en de chocoladefabriek. Nou dat is echt ook heel leuk. Dan kom je samen met Willy Wonka in een hele lege donkere ruimte. En dan ga je stap voor stap zijn hele fantasie fabriek weer opnieuw opbouwen. Ongelooflijk wat daar allemaal in verwerkt zit, de Oempaloempa's en de kinderen die zich niet gehouden hebben aan afspraken, het meisje dat dan veranderd in een grote blauwe bes.

Dat zijn eigenlijk de dingen waar je mee bezig bent, zodat je jezelf en je gedachten even stil kunt zetten.

VOICE-OVER
Zij heeft geleerd hoe ze met de dingen kan omgaan en relativeren, zegt ze.

INGE
Ja, dat heb ik in die twee en een half jaar gedaan dat ik hier zit. Want daarvoor was het gewoon blik op oneindig en maar doorgaan en doorgaan en doorgaan. Je had ook helemaal geen tijd om na te denken.

VOICE-OVER
Corinne startte de stichting, EndParalysis om onderzoek te steunen.

CORINNE

After a few years I started looking to see if there was something that could help me, in terms of research.

VOICE-OVER
After she had to leave her job, she threw herself into this research.

CORINNE

Paralysis itself probably cannot be reversed, or, at least, not fully reversed through just one therapy. It should therefore be approached through a combination of strategies and therapies. That is why research on an international level is very important. But there is hope of real progress and if we can do something about it, then we should.

VOICE-OVER
Around the block is a scattering. Is getting to know your body with every step you take.

As with any line you write. Every level you pass. Every brush stroke.

Around the block is all about going for something, daring to dream hard and at the same time keeping both feet on the ground. It is surrendering to the road ahead, to the path that you do not always choose for yourself.

You find out more about Corinne's foundation EndParalysis here: https://endparalysis.org/?lang=nl

CORINNE
Na een aantal jaar ben ik eigenlijk gaan zoeken of het toch niet iets is wat mij zou kunnen helpen, qua onderzoek.

VOICE-OVER
Toen ze moest stoppen met haar werk stortte ze zich er ten volle op.

CORINNE
Het wordt waarschijnlijk niet geholpen of wordt niet volledig geholpen met alleen één therapie. Het moet een combinatie zijn van strategieën en van therapieën. Daarom is samenwerking op internationaal niveau heel erg belangrijk. Maar er is hoop en er is echt vooruitgang en als wij iets daartegen kunnen doen, dan moeten we het ook doen.

VOICE-OVER
Een blokje om is verstrooiing. Is je lichaam leren kennen bij elke stap die je zet.
Zoals bij elke regel die je schrijft. Elk level dat je passeert. Iedere penseelstreek.
Een blokje om is ergens volledig voor gaan, heel hard durven dromen en tegelijkertijd met je beide benen op de grond blijven staan. Het is je overgeven, aan de weg die voor je ligt, aan het pad waar je niet altijd zelf voor kiest.

Realm – or, Observing the Melting of a Brain

JEANNETTE PETRIK

In September of 2020, Jeannette Petrik was invited to take part in a short residency at Onomatopee. The focus of the residency was to spend time with the street of Lucas Gasselstraat, the street on which Onomatopee has been located since 2019. Jeannette was given complete artistic freedom in how to observe, detail, and respond to the street. The residency aimed to investigate how subjective and personal our experience of place and space can be, and to begin to compile documentation of an area, and particularly a street, that is slowly but surely evolving, and already showing the initial signs of gentrification.

Being tired somehow informed my experience.
Without the dampening effects of the sun I might have been too distracted, or may not have gotten into a meditative state as intuitively. It felt as though the blurred vision sharpened my focus, flattening my perception, helping me see that which was directly in front of me, rather than wandering into complexity, as I was used to.

I'm reminded of a conversation I had years ago, in which we talked about the handling of collective conflicts, struggling to cope with the fact that it often felt impossible to manage disagreements that concerned the collective. Sometimes, people simply shut off and refuse to go further into discussion, only accepting their own perspective as valid.

In this case, we ended up agreeing that the collective needed a sauna and imagined conflicts being taken into discussion after all parties had spent time in the heat together. We imagined melted brains as a good basis for benevolence which would break habits and routines of disagreeing for the sake of 'being right'.
I'm sitting on my sofa, typing "effect of sun exhaustion on cognitive functioning" into the search engine on my laptop. The first result presents a research article published by the European Commission. "Too much sunlight on the head obstructs thinking," it reads. I smile. "A group of researchers has found that direct and prolonged exposure to sunlight impairs motor and cognitive performance."

Walking.
Boredom.
Repetition.

Without confusion, without guidance, I navigate what feels like the periphery of a town, bordering both the center and the residential, industrial outskirts. As though meditating, I wander, investigating whatever normality could mean in this context of parallel realities.

To me, mediocrity means delving into that which isn't exciting. It feels difficult to come up with a clear definition. I'm inclined to use gestures, mimics and sounds to describe my relation to mediocrity: 'Meh' comes to mind.

"*Meh* (/mɛ/) is an interjection used as an expression of indifference or boredom. It is often regarded as a verbal equivalent of a shrug of the shoulders. The use of the term "*meh*" shows that the speaker is apathetic, uninterested, or indifferent to the question or subject at hand. It is occasionally used as an adjective, meaning something is mediocre or unremarkable."

Wikipedia knows what I mean.

My brain had partially melted, I felt. Thus, my perception turned towards elements which I might not have noticed otherwise.

Like a lion in an imaginary cage.

Rather than leaving me physically exhausted I felt that the exposure to the sun slightly altered my perception. Preparing me for opening up my attention, leaving no space for boredom.

I started with an incredibly simple task: walking to the end of the street, then, turning around, walking to the other end of the street.

I walked up and down, curiously, and recorded myself speaking about that which I saw. I felt odd pursuing such a simple task while others around me were working; car dealers stacking up tires in their yard, warehouse workers moving building materials with a forklift, construction site workers on the building site of new houses, technicians installing a mobile antenna on the roof of a warehouse.

I type "is art work?" into the search engine. The first result reads: "Creating art is a valid career. Our culture tends to believe that creating art or music is something that is only reserved for those lucky few who, for whatever reason, have too much time on their hands."

I consider whether the word 'art' was out of place.

This was not a place for strolling around, I felt. This was a place of work, or transit.
Work is a practice I feel ambiguous about, generally.

The kind of work that I was pursuing didn't feel like an appropriate addition to the work that others were doing around here.

Is this a gesture of gentrification? Or, is gentrification primarily linked to property speculation and, thus, less about individual behaviours?

The article continues: "Artists are those whose purpose is not to make us speed up and work faster, but to slow down and notice the beauty that is already around us. Artists who allow us to step outside of ourselves and experience the world from a new perspective. Being an artist is about being willing to listen closely and then doing your best to describe what you find."

I'm slightly bored by these lines, while knowing that there's truth in them. I decide not to continue to review the search results. The question was rhetorical anyway.

I repeated the exercise of walking up and down and shifted my focus with every iteration.

Taking photographs of things that struck me
Looking at materials and evidence of maintenance and wear
Listening to sounds, closing my eyes now and then
Looking on the floor, searching for traces and hints
Looking into buildings, observing people

A scooter, a car, a truck, another car, two people on bikes, a car, a crow, another car, a bike's chain rattling—it could use some oil—tires on asphalt, bike, car, car, car, car, bike, car, truck, car, fork lift, van, a staple gun on air pressure, car, another one, a truck, more staples, a drill, truck, scooter.

I decided not to force anything.
I reacted to spontaneous hunches and impulses.
Discipline had no relevance whatsoever.

The only thing I felt was relevant was walking up and down the street.

Whatever happened while I was walking, or anytime while engaging with the project, became part of my experience.

A sense of honesty.

"What is intuition?" I'm reminded of the TV show Jeopardy!.

Wikipedia describes the word 'intuition' as "the ability to acquire knowledge without recourse to conscious reasoning. The word 'intuition' comes from the Latin verb 'intueri' translated as 'consider' or from the late middle English word 'intuit', 'to contemplate'." Contemplating seems like a word that's appropriate to what I was doing while—I check for the translation of the German word 'flanieren'. Wikipedia directs me to the article about the word 'Flâneur':

"A flâneur is an ambivalent figure of urban affluence and modernity, representing the ability to wander detached from society with no other purpose than to be an acute observer of industrialised, contemporary life."

The decadent undertone overpowers the attempt of a neutral description: "The word carried a set of rich associations: an emblematic archetype of the urban, modern (even modernist) experience."

I hear tires thrown into the back of a van.

The collective encyclopedia continues to describe: "The term has acquired an additional architecture and urban planning sense, referring to passers-by who experience incidental or intentional psychological effects from the design of a structure." I can relate this phenomenon to my experience on Lucas Gasselstraat. Its 'design' has most probably had an effect on my psyche.

I pick up a phonecall while walking.

The conversation with my friend Marie helped inform the experience I had. We talked about the word 'punk' and what it meant to us. While the term does feel relevant to both of us, we agreed that we don't fully identify as punks. Somehow, the term feels antiquated if used uncommented, we felt, and potentially contemporary if we updated its definition.

Marie sent me a comic which she had found in a zine at 56a, an anarchist infoshop in London some time ago. She told me that she had shared the drawing with her mothers who couldn't believe that the word punk was still relevant to people of our generation.

The comic showed five characters who all seemed to identify with the word 'punk' and described their relation to different facets of the term, ranging from anti-establishment attitudes, ideas of social change and political struggle, prioritising workers' rights, hedonism, creative strategies and fashion. We were not sure which facets we identified with specifically, since their depictions were stereotypical and overly simplified. Still, the comic made a point: punk is many things.

Doing whatever I felt like was freeing.
There were no expectations, not even from myself.

The complete freedom to explore demonstrated a contrast to what I usually do, even though I haven't directly felt unfree in a long time.

Freedom is a relational sensation. So is empowerment.

I'm reminded of a text I read years ago, within which Zizek talks about the distinctive characteristics of an invisibility of oppression within Capitalism.

Maybe punk means reacting to the invisible lack of freedom.

I picked up a book about invisible writing.

'Invisibility' strikes me as a complex notion. When a choice, I see how it can be comforting to feel less pressure and attention from others. When not a choice, being invisibile can feel like a punishment. I type the word 'invisibility' into the search engine. One of the first results is a person's description of invisibility as a superpower: "I realise that being low profile means I can reach out and get involved in more things. It also means that I have been drawn to others who also are quietly trying to bring about change. A benefit is being able to see what others do not."

I watched a video within which a person spoke about their experiences both as a farmer and as a student in Thailand. They had decided to choose a life which they felt made them the happiest: a life which wasn't overly complex. They described that their experiences of institutions and academic egos felt complicated and oppositional to happiness.

I'm reminded of Stefan Sagmeister who presents his career as something based upon his path towards happiness.

Maybe happiness is something that feels easy.
I'm sitting outside to eat. There's new laundry hung on
the roof terrace opposite. A circular saw in the
background. A person with a bag from the close-by super-
market crosses the street in front of me, wearing
working clothes. Children screaming, crying, squeaking.
Birds. Cars accelerating. A rope hitting a flagpole
regularly in the wind. A vintage road bike, a vespa, a
Mercedes. Two people in suits walking, one of them
on the phone, the other looking into windows, occasionally
stopping. A group of teenagers on bikes.

I often feel overwhelmed by my senses. I've noticed that
I'm typically more sensitive to stimuli than others around me.
This sometimes feels like a superpower, and like a curse just as
often.

The only real cure to feeling overwhelmed that I've found
so far is limiting my focus, concentrating on something that feels
easy—breathing, moving, feeling, meditating or a combination
thereof, depending on what feels easiest in a situation.

I type the word 'sensory' into the search engine,
not knowing how to specify my search and complete the
request. I check the suggested searches. The first suggested
result, meaning, the most searched for is 'sensory processing
sensitivity'.

For about a year, I've been studying and practicing full
presence meditation after Danis Bois, who takes mindfulness as
a basis for discovering one's emotional state and dispositions.
Practicing meditation has taught me to consciously place focus;
beginning with the act of sitting, of consciously closing my
eyes, remaining immobile and listening in to the silence within me
and around me.
I had issues with listening to silence for a while as I
couldn't get over its oxymoronic nature. Eventually, I started to
view silence as empty space and could focus on the empty
space that surrounds things, noises, people and thoughts.
A contrast builds up the more clear the distinction between empty space and things becomes.

My thoughts turn into noise.

I search for "what distinguishes noise from" and complete the search request with the automated suggestion "what distinguishes noise from music in the presence of". I'm not quite sure what the phrase "the presence of" points towards exactly but I'm curious to discover the search results. I find an online quiz about sound, which begins with a test for basic knowledge about the mechanics of sound waves and, eventually, brings up a question which corresponds with the search request: "What most distinguishes noise from music in the presence of" - the answer being "regularity". 'Repetition,' I think in response.

Noise intrigues me. I wonder what distinguishes noise and order, noise and music, noise and sound. I understand order as seeing patterns within landscapes of noise. Noise is unfamiliar and disorganised, possibly unexpected and unwanted. In other words, noise is chaotic. When thinking about music, noise becomes sounds that are outside of one's control, mostly not deliberate and undesired; the cracking sound of a vinyl record playing or the skipping of a scratched disc, a microphone's feedback or the humming sound of an amplifier. I often think of noise as sound but visual noise works similarly.

Unexpected revelations suddenly pop up: the children only scream in the mornings, the street is busiest at 7am, the decorative flags are taken off the monster truck wheel every night, the 50s/60s/70s warehouse is just a wall, plants grow wildly outside of designated areas.

My sight has become one of my body's weak points. When I'm tired or stressed, I'm easily overwhelmed by visual triggers such as bright lights and saturated colours and tend to react with agitation to noisy visual stimuli.

Again, I seek to quench my curiosity and make a search request: "noisy visual stimuli." The title of a search result intrigues me, as it reads: "How the Visual Cortex Handles Stimulus Noise: Insights from Amblyopia." I don't know what Amblyopia is.

I'm directed to an article in a scientific journal. Its abstract reads: "Adding noise to a visual image makes object recognition more effortful and has a widespread effect on human electrophysiological responses. However, visual cortical processes directly involved in handling the stimulus noise have yet to be identified and dissociated from the modulation of the neural responses due to the deteriorated structural information and increased stimulus uncertainty in the case of noisy images." The abstract goes on to describe the study and its findings in more detail than I can understand.

Next to the abstract, there's a collection of diagrams and graphics which are there to illustrate the results of the study the article describes. I don't understand the meaning of any of the figures or numbers and can't come to draw any conclusions from the paper. I lose interest.

Eventually, I don't feel
like walking anymore
I sit and watch and hear.
the buzzing sound of a scooter
a car driving by, a truck's motor
in the distance, another car
two people on their bikes, a
female voice speaking Dutch
single words, a car, a crow,

a car, the tires of a bike on
the asphalt, a car turning and
accelerating, a truck speeding,
stopping, a car, a fork lift,
squeaking sounds, the slamming
of a car's door, a van, a staple

gun on air pressure, irregular,
hand-held, a car speeding past
another car, a truck arriving
more staples, many more, a drill,
a crane moving,
a circular saw in the distance.

I enter the building and close the door. I watch the short film 'The Neighbor's Window'. It ends with a sequence of credits and street sounds.

Zooming in, witnessing the unexpected, navigating noise:

The sun is harsh, again.
I manage to zone out easily.

The broken rhythm of a rope regularly
hitting the flag pole on the building opposite,
cars, now and then, maybe a bike
somebody is playing with their keys.

Sounds separate into layers.

A person on a cargo bike wears
the uniform of a postal delivery service
singing loudly. Magpies communicate
from one roof to another.

A person on a mobility scooter,
the seat squeaks, the motor
sounds exhausted. A child cries
loudly, whaling whining sounds.

A fried brain turns noise into less of a distraction and more of a thing of attention.

I continue to watch a talk by Jon Jandai.
"If you have a lot of time you have time to be with yourself. Then you have time to understand yourself and to understand what you want for your life. Anybody has a choice. A choice to be easy or a choice to be hard."

After a few days, I notice that I'm more easily distracted and need more rest.

I take a nap.

As a last search for today I type the words "importance of napping" and find a list of search results which are displayed together with excerpts that all sound similar. Their essence, at first glance: naps are good.

The word 'good' feels appallingly mediocre.

Scattered noise.
Zooming in.
Lucid Dreaming.

205

NATURE BOY, SWIM GOOD

ANNEE GRØTTE VIKEN

There was a boy
A very strange, enchanted boy
They say he wandered very far, very far
Over land and sea
A little shy and sad of eye
But very wise was he[1]

(TO WITNESS)
To see something happen, especially an accident or crime[2]

He sat in the living room while he tied his dotted black and navy-blue trainers. Laces in place he leaned forward on his well-seasoned armchair and observed how the wind and rain moved in erratic throws, transforming his glass door into a terrific cymbal. The gutter doubled up as a xylophone and together they presented quite the performance. He tapped his fingers on the leather of the chair, inhaled deeply and reached for the handle.

I see his naked feet and raise the tide by two degrees. As
he enters, I close around his legs and swallow them in sync
with his pace. The subtle strength of my mass grabs
hold of his joints, and my fluid, which he may experience as
freezing cold, pins itself to his flesh and directs a sensa-
tion similar to a million needles puncturing his skin. As he
stabilizes, I tap into the muscular tissues and massage
my flow into his breath and simmer softly; - Inhabit yourself
so your joints don't freeze solid and break with a tap on
the shoulder. Submerge and enter my belly. Step onto the
soft yellow brick road below and rest assured that you
have been here before.

I watch as he lowers his torso, takes a deep breath, and
sends oxygen into his blood. Pumping consciousness into
being, the oxygen enters his body, every limb, every vein,
and every cell.

When I sigh you are reminded of my piercing strength.
I stroke your arms up close; bricks become stones and
stones grains of sand holding your feet in place.
Solids and fluids tickle your soles as the sunrise colours
my surface. Breathe. The brick road slopes with each ebb.

*Look to the fading moon for directions, words won't
do much, opening your mouth is a bad idea. I advise you
to keep your mask in place. Without doing this, you
might drown in your own vocal folds. Here, the body is
your language, exert energy and create vibrations. I read
them all.*

(TO HAPPEN)
*When a place or period witnesses a particular event, the event
happens in that place or during that period*

Fully submerged, he was greeted by a deafening silence. The darkness was complete and a mild current guided him towards the
soft yellow glow of neatly arranged bricks. Eager to close in
on the enigmatic image bobbing up ahead, he pushed forward
but was quickly stalled. There was no rushing. Moving was
different. He thought of Buzz Aldrin and his mobility test on the
moon. One foot to the side for making turns; kangaroo jumps
work, but the traditional 'one foot after the other' is less exhausting. He swayed and fell off the side of the road before he
regained his balance and stepped back onto the bricks. From the
depths below jellyfish streetlights scintillated with a dark
green light emanating an electric beauty that mirrored Chopin's
seductive nocturnes racing across the keys. Every breath
was hauntingly present, like a river rushing past on repeat. Steady
rhythms took a hold of his hand and guided his moves, one
after the other. Lobsters, eels and oysters surveyed him from afar
as the current dropped him off at their dilapidated golden
city gate. White neon circulated; *the weather is sponsored by
Qatar Airways and Bloomberg reports that Water© now trades
on the stock exchange.* A wheezing sound was carried through
narrow alleys and into the main waterways where it merged with
endless pastel-coloured streams of soothing aqua pop. The circular city was waking to the first tide and streetlamps floated
past in translucent nightgowns, flickering gently as they ducked
behind skeleton reefs. Exhalation keeps the circulation going.
The city flows, rushes, washes, breaks, and freezes over. He
found the forced slowness confusing and was scared by the way
it changed his perception.

A blizzard of white, orange, and yellow flakes hurled across the
street into the wide, open mouth of the ocean, silently screaming

in the narrow, empty space hunched between the bustling crowds passing on the sidewalk and the solitary hearts beating softly in the dark backyard. The flakes, released on cue, every year at the same time from the lunar cycle, were eggs, sent into existence when the temperature is just right. Entire colonies of reefs had been synced and released simultaneously, en massing their future selves into the world. Billions born in a colourful cascade, now released into being the very moment the ocean filled her lungs in the empty arcade. *Don't you want somebody to love? Don't you need somebody to love?* Her voice ricocheted the new-borns back into the streets and a colourful bundle swirled and made a precise throw against his face as he turned the corner. Her scream howled into his ears conjointly with the song of a children's choir, lining the steps next to him. The kids bellowed out with tremendous joy and their vibration merged with the scream and gave birth to a haunting harmony pulsating past loudspeakers, fences, bulls and horses, and into the city's marrow of stone.

The vibrations rang violently in his head. He had seen them; they had been everywhere; like snow. Rapid pulsations rose from his lips and the buds egressed as air bubbles. The tiny capsules displayed time beautifully as they rose slowly before his eyes towards the surface. The absence and presence of time was a measurement he didn't fully understand and therefore could not entirely decipher. But what he did know was that time spent, physically or mentally, translated into space, and that he had been born in the depths of it, and so had the sea.

(TO SHOW)
To present or give proof of something

> -Are you sure about that tree?
> – What do you...
> - Can we agree that it has shed its leaves?
> - Uh, yes
> - Can we agree that the leaves that are shed cover the ground?
> - Yes
> - Can we agree that it is unruly?
> - ...well, leaves...fall
> - Let me rephrase, can we control the process of falling?

- Well... no... but
- So, can we agree that it is unruly?
- Eh yes, but...
- Thank you, that was all I wanted to know.

After the ground melted beneath your burning feet there was no way back. The nestled world didn't have a choice, what I cared for below destroyed me from above, but I will still hold your raft, I'll even push it forward. Don't give me those ocean eyes; it's true. My body holding the city is a collective, urban blind spot.

I know it is difficult to slow down, but there is no way around it. If you don't, my grip will tighten, and the dance will darken. One restless turn and you will be out. Balance is key in this town. Too much will cause you to levitate and too little will give you a blackout and collapse you into the depths of my being where none of your kind has ever been before. The mind is as flexible as the challenges it receives, and my streets trace their own existence. When your surroundings turn into one unidentifiable mass their components become invisible to you. Neon signs look good in a haze of waves but hold no real answers, they point to solutions where there are none to be found. On a perfect porch nothing clouds the view.
You have been courageous to come inside.

He ran into the rain with his headlamp tightened around his grey woollen hat and watched as millions of stars suddenly raced towards him, each drop reflecting another galaxy. He sped up; outside there was nothing but endless deep space. A row of poplar trees bowed their crowns in return as the city woke to another season. Nature Boy wasn't given well-rounded eyes to perceive the world as flat.

I'm about to drive in the ocean
I'ma try to swim from somethin' bigger than me
Kick off my shoes
And swim good, and swim good

Take off this suit
And swim good, and swim good, good[3]

The greatest thing you'll ever learn
Is just to love and be loved in return[1]

Our cities were born from the ocean and the origins of our oceans are in the stars. "It's a rare gift, to know where you need to be, before you've been to all the places you don't need to be." Ursula K. Le Guin, Tales of Earthsea. With a rise in temperature of 2 degrees, all coral reefs in the world will die. They inhabit only 1% of the world's oceans but 25% of marine life depends on them. In addition to altering the air we all breathe, an estimated 775 million people are highly dependent on marine ecosystems . Up to 60 % of the adult human body is water. We are one. As biologist and former Mayor of Hawaii, Jeremy Harris writes, "Oceans and cities are inexorably linked and saving our oceans is an urban challenge." [4]

[1]
Nature Boy, Nat King Cole (eden ahbez)

[2]
*Witnessing definition –
https://dictionary.cambridge.org/
dictionary/english/witnessing*

[3]
*Swim Good, Nostalgia, ULTRA,
Frank Ocean*

[4]
*Further resources
https://www.gdrc.org/oceans/Cities%
20and%20Oceans%20PDF.doc
https://www.un.org/depts/los/oceans_
foundation.htm*

*https://www.usgs.gov/special-topic/
water-science-school/science/water-
you-water-and-human-body?qt-
science_center_objects=0#qt-
science_center_objects*

*https://www.nasa.gov/specials/
ocean-worlds/*

*https://conbio.onlinelibrary.wiley.com/
doi/10.1111/conl.12617*

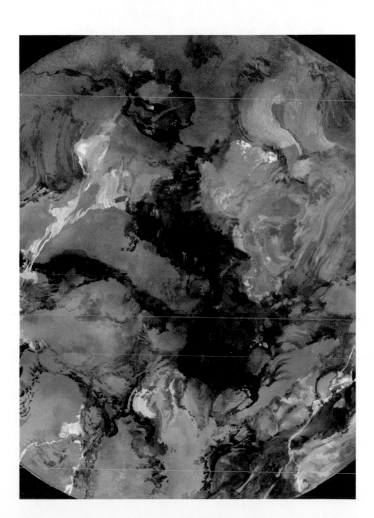

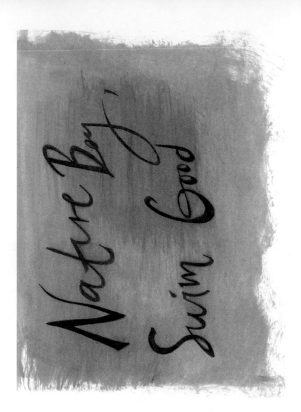

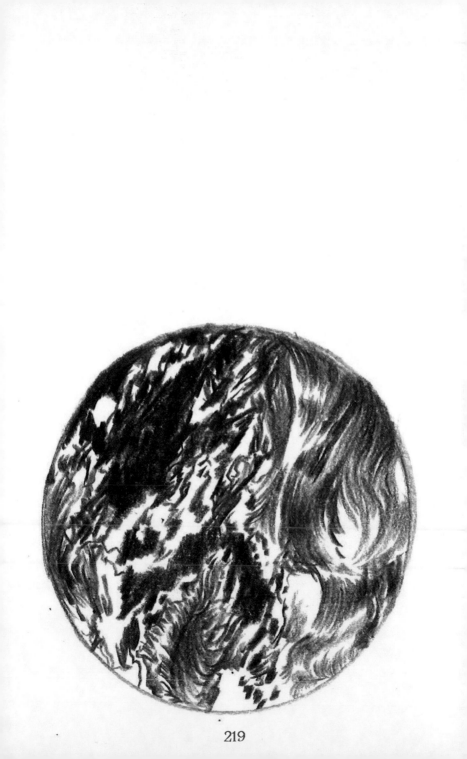

End Note

As mentioned in the Introduction to this publication, the period in which *Rights of Way* was developed and produced also played host to a number of events that have since permanently shifted our individual and collective perceptions of, and relationships to, public space. Alongside this, our awareness of the privileges and fears we embody and embrace when present in these spaces have been increasingly heightened. We have been witnesses to horrific and senseless acts of violence that have led us to question who, including ourselves, is truly safe, truly accepted, and can truly feel at home and welcomed, in the public domain. These have all been questions without clear, linear answers, that have been with us for generations, and will continue to shape our lives and lived experiences for generations to come. It is clear that as public space, and its rights of access evolve, so too will the opportunities and challenges presented to us through our own individual experiences, and as part of wider societal shifts.

The hope is that instead of providing direct answers, the texts collected in this publication offer new ways of thinking, approaching, and *being* in public space. They interrogate how public space is intrinsically linked to our public consciousness, public lives, and public histories, and, together, they showcase that we all hold within us the possibility to be witnesses and activators of our cities and spaces, bodily and otherwise. For that reason, as Rebecca Solnit so astutely states, the movements of our bodies around cities and spaces, continue to be "the most obvious and obscure thing in the world".[1]

I want to share my gratitude for all of the artists and writers that have contributed to the *Rights of Way* exhibition and publication: Pauline Agustoni, Elia Castino, The Dazzle Club, Shannon Finnegan, Kevin Gotkin, Annee Grøtte Viken, Christa-Maria Lerm-Hayes, Corinne Heyrman, Paoletta Holst, Rahma

Khazam, Alessandro Marchi, Jeannette Petrik and Soeria van den Wijngaard, it has truly been a pleasure. Thank you to Studio Bramesfeld for the wonderful and inspiring designs and visual cues provided throughout the project. Finally, to those who have supported in a multitude of ways in the shaping and formation of this project: Andy Norstrom, Ailyn Mercedes-Manchego, Wibke Bramesfeld, Joannette van der Veer, Demi van Venrooij, Quentin Gaudry, and Maria Morales, thank you.

[1]
Rebecca Solnit *Wanderlust: A History of Walking*, Granta Books 2014

Biographies

Chrɪsta-Marɪa Lerm Hayes is Professor of Modern and Contemporary Art History, University of Amsterdam and academic director of the Amsterdam School for Heritage, Memory and Material Culture. Until 2014 she was Professor of Iconology, University of Ulster in Belfast, where she led a Research Graduate School. She studied in Heidelberg, London and Cologne, where she gained her PhD (researched as James Joyce Foundation Scholar, Zurich). She held an Irish Research Council Post-Doctoral Fellowship at UCD.

Her research focuses on word and image studies, visual legacies of (Irish) writers, performance, the historiography of art and curation. Rooted in Joseph Beuys studies, she is interested in social practices, post-War art histories, performance, and art research.

Her books include: *Brian O'Doherty/Patrick Ireland: Word, Image and Institutional Critique* (ed., Valiz 2017); *Post-War Germany and 'Objective Chance': W.G. Sebald, Joseph Beuys and Tacita Dean (Steidl 2011); James Joyce als Inspirationsquelle für Joseph Beuys*(Olms 2001); and *Joyce in Art* (Lilliput 2004).

She has curated at: Royal Hibernian Academy and Goethe Institut, Dublin; Tolstoy Estate, Russia; MoA, Seoul National University, Korea; Golden Thread Gallery, Belfast; LCGA, Limerick; CCI, Paris; Maagdenhuis, University of Amsterdam; M HKA, Antwerp, and the VanAbbemuseum, Eindhoven.

The Dazzle Club explores surveillance in public space. Through embodied performance, moving image and digital interventions, they draw awareness to technological bias and contested data collection, and build new expressions of trust.

The Dazzle Club is a collaboration between four artists, Georgina Rowlands, Emily Roderick, Evie Price and Anna Hart. It began in August 2019 in response to the forced admission that facial recognition technology was being used by developer Argent on the King's Cross Estate in London, a place in which they have all made art for many years. As citizens of a heavily surveilled city, second only to Beijing in density of cameras per resident, they lead monthly artist-led silent walks with participants wearing CV Dazzle, a technique originally developed by researcher Adam Harvey. Their embodied research has been featured widely in national and international media including Vogue, Reuters, BBC, I-D, and The Observer. Recent exhibitions/

events include *Screen Walks* with Photographers' Gallery and Fotomuseum Winterthur, *MASCARAS* at Galeria Municipal do Porto, *!!!Sección Arte*, Cuba.

Rahma Khazam is a Paris-based researcher, critic and art historian. She received her Ph.D. from the Sorbonne in aesthetics and art theory. Her research spans the fields of contemporaneity, modernism, image theory, and speculative realism and has been published in edited volumes and academic journals. She has also written catalogue essays, articles and exhibition reviews on the work of artists ranging from Paul Panhuysen to Christina Kubisch. In 2017, she received the AICA France Art Criticism Award and in 2019, she contributed the essay "Genre and Gender" to *Hidden Alliances* (ed. Elisabeth Schimana, Hatje Cantz), an edited volume exploring the role of women composers in avant-garde music.

Elia Castino engages with space making and art practice.
He explores the architecture of the everyday as spatial dimension and cultural construct.
His work questions the conventional domestic connotation of the home by staging scenarios that present another idea of inhabiting. His narrative occurs at the threshold between reverie and reality, intimacy and exposure.
He studied at Politecnico di Milano and UCA Canterbury and he holds a Master Degree from Studio for Immediate Spaces, Sandberg Instituut. He is currently based in Amsterdam.

Pauline Agustoni is a concept designer who works for society and culture. She has a special interest in "forgotten" narratives—those of minority groups, old traditional know-hows, or everyday overlooked actions—and uses her projects as a way to tell those stories and answer the questions that emerge from the process.
She values a diverse choice of media and techniques in her work. For every project, the medium is reflected on and determined by the research theme and working method. Beyond the materials, what bridges all her projects is her commitment in addressing social, historical and cultural issues. That's the reason

why collaboration and exchange are at the core of her practice, which is fed by in-depth interactions with the affected audience.

Pauline is based in Berlin, Germany. After graduating from Design Academy Eindhoven in the Netherlands in 2019, she developed her own artistic practice, working with media such as conceptual, textile and object design, installation, and publication.

Kevin Gotkin is an access ecologist, community organizer, and teacher. They received their PhD from the University of Pennsylvania in 2018 and were a Visiting Assistant Professor of Media, Culture, & Communication at NYU from 2018–2021. From 2016–2019, they co-founded Disability/Arts/NYC with Simi Linton. More recently, they were an Artist-in-Residence at Het HEM in the Netherlands, lead steward of the REMOTE ACCESS nightlife series, and an inaugural cohort member of Creative Time's Think Tank.

Shannon Finnegan is an artist. Some of their recent work includes *Anti-Stairs Club Lounge*, an ongoing project that gathers people together who share an aversion to stairs; *Alt-Text as Poetry*, a collaboration with Bojana Coklyat that explores the expressive potential of image description; and *Do You Want Us Here or Not*, a series of benches and cushions designed for exhibition spaces. They have done projects with Banff Centre, ARGOS Centre for Audiovisual Arts, the High Line, the Museum of Contemporary Art Denver, and Nook Gallery. Their work has been supported by a 2018 Wynn Newhouse Award, a 2019 residency at Eyebeam, and a 2020 grant from Art Matters Foundation.

Working as an artist, architectural researcher and writer based in Brussels, *Paoletta Holst's* practice operates at the intersection of different disciplines to investigate the social, historical and political dimension of architecture and the urban environment. She is interested in the influence of formal spatial/political power structures of our living environment, and in the informal counter-strategies people create to deal with them. In 2016/2017 she was a Jan van Eyck participant, and since

2018 she has been working with different people and in different formations on projects around the colonial history of the Netherlands in Indonesia. In 2019 she participated in the 900mdpl biennale in Kaliurang, Indonesia. Together with Paolo Patelli she currently works on an archival research project rethinking the 'logic' of the Tillema Collections, collaborating with Research Center for Material Culture, the Eye Filmmuseum, and the Institute of Beeld en Geluid.

Together with Rob Ritzen she founded That Might Be Right, an artistic and socially engaged organization dedicated to researching, developing and supporting alternatives to the present. Since 2017 she has been teaching history and theory of architecture at the Rotterdam Academy of Architecture and since 2018 has been working as an editor for the online platform Archined.

Soeria van den Wijngaard (NL, 1996) is a multi-media sound artist. She creates active listening experiences and immersive installations that revolve around deep listening, activation of the parasympathetic nervous system, personal integration, and embodiment. She strives to make accessible and sustainable work that invites authenticity in all ages. In doing so, she hopes to inaugurate new neurological pathways into a compassionate sensitivity towards self and others in relation to the external world. Her latest work *Witness What Remains* is an immersive listening installation that invites visitors of all ages and backgrounds to interact, explore and play with 300 ceramic sound pieces dispersed in space. Slowly, one becomes aware of the sound-story playing in the space; voices fade as the room turns into a loud thunder- and rainstorm. The fieldrecordings of this installation are based on a true story of a neighbour in Sparta, Greece. We misunderstood her aggressive behavior. The installation asks: *How could we listen more compassionately to each other?*

Soeria graduated from the ArtScience Interfaculty of the Royal Conservatory and The Royal Academy of Arts in The Hague (2020). She followed courses at the Sonology Department and fell deeply in love with fieldrecording and deep listening. Next to her art practice, she has been practicing Usui Reiki and yoga since 2012. In 2018 and 2020 she respectively obtained her 200-hour yoga and Reiki I certificates. This combination of interests in art, listening and holistic living has resulted in a specific body of work that intertwines the two practices. She has performed and exhibited at Onomatopee Projects, The Grey Space In The Middle, The Wave Field Synthesis Festival, Operator Radio, Beyond The Audible Symposium, Helicopter, de Besturing, Sonic Acts Academy and Resonance FM. She co-created and hosted "Growing Pains", a monthly embodied transformative justice workshop for activist artists with Leyla Benouniche.

Alessandro Marchi is an Italian artist based in Oslo, Norway. Marchi's artist practice revolves around human modified landscape, identity, self reflection, chaos and public space, especially how humans constantly negotiate and modify the space they live in. He works experimentally and site specifically to create installations, events, artist books, walks, sculptures, carpets, paintings, maps, texts and audio pieces. Marchi holds an MFA at the Oslo National Academy of the Arts (2020) and an MSC in Mechanical Engineering at the Universitá degli Studi di Bologna (2002).

Jeannette Petrik is a cultural producer with a diverse practice which oscillates between creative, journalistic and academic writing, experimental noise and music, two-dimensional visual production, squatting, building and community organising. Interested in phenomena at the social fringes and cultural peripheries, as well as meditation, bodywork and acrobatics, Petrik values radical, honest and critical attitudes which challenge notions of normality.

Jeannette Petrik considers language and design as an opportunity for public empowerment and skill sharing, and as a tool for everyday politics. Within their work, an in-depth analysis of the dynamics inherent in social arrangements and material cultures is often the basis for the creation of intersectional geographies. Putting into doubt our socio-ontological constants, our discursive and material routines, which structure our lifeworlds and necessitates us to explore a mode of thought which cuts across convenient totalisations. Petrik is dedicated to the facilitation of events of doubt in dialogue with her surrounding environment. After graduating from a BA in Product Design at Central Saint Martins in London, UK, she pursued an MA in

Contextual Design at the Design Academy Eindhoven, NL, and has been self-employed since.

Corinne Heyrman (1994) studied word art in Antwerp. She writes prose and non-fiction, makes theater and radio. Corinne was a writer-in-residence at Duizel in the Park and has performed for Lowlands and Oerol, among others. Her work relates in all forms to society and the question of how art can contribute to this. In November 2018, Wintertuin Publishers published her chapbook Mogelijke eigenschappen, in which she investigates research. Corinne regularly makes shows and performances. In the autumn of 2019, she made the performance When my father was still a guest worker with Het Zuidelijk Toneel. As a podcast maker, she contributes to Radio Kras, De Bijsluiter and Drie uur 's nachts. She is currently working on her debut novel, which will be published by De Arbeiderspers.

Corinne Heyrman (1994) studeerde Woordkunst in Antwerpen. Ze schrijft proza en non-fictie, maakt theater en radio. Corinne was writer-in-residence bij Duizel in het Park en droeg voor op onder andere Lowlands en Oerol. Haar werk verhoudt zich in alle vormen tot de maatschappij en de vraag hoe kunst daar iets aan kan bijdragen. In november 2018 verscheen bij Wintertuin Uitgeverij haar chapbook *Mogelijke eigenschappen*, waarin zij het onderzoeken onderzoekt. Corinne maakt regelmatig voorstellingen en performances. Ze maakte in de herfst van 2019 met Het Zuidelijk Toneel de voorstelling *Toen mijn vader nog een gastarbeider was*. Als podcastmaker werkt ze mee aan Radio Kras, De Bijsluiter en Drie uur 's nachts. Momenteel werkt zij aan haar debuutroman die bij De Arbeiderspers zal verschijnen.

Annee Grøtte Viken (NO) lives and works between Norway and Brussels (BE).
Explores how fiction can function as a tool for approaching, understanding and making space with special attention to materials, cultural heritage and ecology. Grøtte Viken has published a book on the subject of 'spaces in fiction' (It Had Something To Do With The Telling Of Time, Onomatopee). Graduate of the Immediate Spaces, Sandberg Instituut and former resident

at the Jan van Eyck Academie in Maastricht as the collaborative practice, Albergo Rosa with architect Maximiliaan Royakkers. Grøtte Viken holds a specialisation in the craft of decorative painting from Van der Kelen Logelain in Brussels, works with artisans, storytelling and heritage in her hometown while currently pursuing a post-master at the Royal Academy of Arts in Stockholm. Teaches creative writing at ArteZ Academy of the Arts (NL), climbs and collects rocks.

Wibke Bramesfeld is an independent graphic and communication designer, based in Rotterdam, NL. Wibke studied at the Peter Behrens School of Arts in Düsseldorf, DE (2012—2016), HDK - Academy of Design and Crafts, Göteborg, SE (2014—2015), and received her MA from the department 'Information Design' at Design Academy Eindhoven, NL, in 2019. Since then she has been running her own design practice 'Studio Bramesfeld'. The studio focuses on book design, visual communication, and graphic identities, across the cultural field at large. The approach of Studio Bramesfeld's work is not only to create visually stimulating designs, but to also build conceptually strong foundations, by taking elements such as graphic design, typography, colour, and materials into consideration for each individual project. The studio has worked in collaboration with many cultural organisations and art publishers, including Valiz, nai010, Archiprix, Design Academy Eindhoven, Onomatopee Projects, and PrintRoom.

Amy Gowen is a curator, writer, and editor living in Rotterdam. She graduated from the MA Arts and Society at Utrecht University in 2019, and previously worked at Onomatopee Projects as City Curator and Publications Editor, where she initiated the *Meeting Grounds* public programme and publication series and curated the *Rights of Way* exhibition. She now works as a programmer for the International Community Arts Festival in Rotterdam, and as publications manager for the School of Commons in Zürich, Switzerland, where she was also a 2021 READ research fellow.

Colophon

Onomatopee 195

Rights of Way
The body as witness
in public space

ISBN: 978-94-93148-70-3

EDITOR
Amy Gowen

CONTRIBUTING AUTHORS
Christa-Maria Lerm-Hayes
The Dazzle Club
Rahma Khazam
Elia Castino
Pauline Agustoni
Kevin Gotkin
Shannon Finnegan
Paoletta Holst
Soeria van den Wijngaard
Alessandro Marchi
Corinne Heyrman
Jeannette Petrik
Annee Grøtte Viken

GRAPHIC DESIGN
Studio Bramesfeld
bramesfeld.com

FONTS
Avara Bold & Bold Italic
Söhne Buch & Buch Kursiv

PAPER
Cover: Munken Lynx 240gr
Inside: G-Print 80gr

PRINTER
Printon, Tallinn

IMAGE CREDITS
Cover & p. 132: Wibke Bramesfeld
p. 27: Aisling O'Beirn, *Some Things About Belfast*, in Space Shuttle, Six Projects of Urban Creativity and Inclusion, Mission Three: North Street / Waring Street (Belfast)', curated by PS² , 20.09–05.10.2006
p. 46–49: Dazzle Club
p. 63–71: Elia Castino
p. 76–94: Pauline Agustoni
p. 115–127: Maria Baranova
p. 167–170: Alessandro Marchi
p. 205–207: Jeannette Petrik
p. 216–219: The Last Whole Earth Catalogue, 1972, editor Stewart Brand.

MADE POSSIBLE BY
Mondriaan Fonds
Province of Noord-Brabant
Cultuur Eindhoven

mondriaan fund   Provincie Noord-Brabant

ϲcultuur
ϲeindhoven